Always There

Always There

Reflections for Moms on God's Presence

Susan Besze Wallace

Revell
a division of Baker Publishing Group
Grand Rapids, Michigan

© 2012 by MOPS International

Published by Revell
a division of Baker Publishing Group
P.O. Box 6287, Grand Rapids, MI 49516-6287
www.revellbooks.com

Printed in the United States of America

Library of Congress Cataloging-in-Publication Data
Wallace, Susan Besze, 1969–
    Always there : reflections for moms on God's presence / Susan Besze Wallace.
      p. cm.
    ISBN 978-0-8007-2116-9 (pbk.)
    1. Meditations. 2. Mothers—Religious life. I. Title.
    BV4529.18.W35 2012
    242′.6431—dc23
                                        2011046573

The internet addresses, email addresses, and phone numbers in this book are accurate at the time of publication. They are provided only as a resource; Baker Publishing Group does not endorse them or vouch for their content or permanence.

Published in association with the literary agency of Alive Communications, Inc., 7680 Goddard Street, Suite 200, Colorado Springs, Colorado 80920, www.alivecommunications.com.

To *all* the moms who poured out their hearts
and to those who do so every day.

Contents

Finding Him   9

1. Dawn: God Is with Us . . . in the Firsts   13

2. Matching Socks: God Is with Us . . . in the
   Mundane   31

3. Duty Calls: God Is with Us . . . in Our Sacrifices   49

4. Holding Hands: God Is with Us . . . in Our
   Marriages   67

5. In the Dark: God Is with Us . . . and in Control   85

6. Girl Power: God Is with Us . . . in Our
   Friendships   103

7. Time Out: God Is with Us . . . When We Feel
   Overwhelmed   121

8. On the Move: God Is with Us . . . in Our Work   143

9. Monkey Bars and Cardboard Cars: God Is with Us
   . . . in Laughter and Play   161

10. Nourishment: God Is with Us . . . and Provides   179

Contributors   197

Acknowledgments   204

Finding Him

.

Yet I am always with you;
you hold me by my right hand.

Psalm 73:23

When I am armed with only a hair dryer, the cascade of my thoughts starts to fall steadily.

The friend I haven't talked to in a while. The need to work with my toddler on writing his letters. The work idea. The warmth of my mother's eyes. The brainstorm for the second grade talent show. The room I need to disinfect. The selfish way I tried to fend off husbandly advances last night during dinner-making, annoyed, before allowing myself to be hugged.

Sometimes I weary of my merry-go-round of a mind. I used to think that if God were involved in these thoughts, it could only be in laughing at how my thoughts resemble a game of dodge ball.

Motherhood has taught me otherwise.

For those ten minutes with the dryer, I am still. Captive to vanity (or necessity, if you could see what my hair looks like if it dries on its own), I drown out all other sounds save those in my head and heart.

For a while, it was the only place I gave God a chance.

He isn't laughing at me. He is leading me. Toward that friend, toward patience, toward priorities. He was just waiting for me to hear him and realize that he is right there, in all the nooks and crannies of the busy, exhausting, and exhilarating job of being a mom. Of being me.

He's in it all, and not just when we choose to thank him or plead with him.

It's one thing to know, in your mind, that God is everywhere. It's another to feel, in your soul, that he is in your everything.

It's easier to feel him when you are holding a delicious, sleeping baby than when you are forced to walk through Target with a smear on your shirt from a public diaper change gone awry. But God is with us in both the rocker and the rocky.

The question is whether we are acknowledging him. And how our lives would change if we were constantly aware that we don't do anything alone.

Throughout the Bible we are shown examples of God communicating with his people. God spoke to Joseph in dreams (see Gen. 37). He spoke to Moses through a burning bush (see Exod. 3). Adam and Eve heard God's voice when they were hiding from him in the garden, afraid because of the bad choice they'd made (see Gen. 2). David heard directly from God when he asked him where he should go (see 2 Sam. 2).

Drought or flood, God was there. Whether they were experiencing new life or retching in guilt or grief, he was there. And between those extremes, in whatever "normal" was, he was there too.

God still speaks to his children, and certainly his children's mothers, in a variety of ways. Seeking him is the surest way to be aware of his presence. Whether it's in prayer, serving his people, reading his Word, or calling out ungracefully in a moment of total maternal madness, we are told to "come boldly unto the throne of grace, that we may obtain mercy, and find grace to help in time of need" (Heb. 4:16 KJV).

Many of the devotions in this book represent such coming before the throne. For some, it was falling down in front of it, as motherhood can bring us to our knees often—and for so many reasons!

My hope is that through reflecting on the words of other moms and the words of the Bible you will be encouraged to find God in the daily. He's with us at the hair dryer and the clothes dryer, in our firsts and our frustrations, in moments of great joy and great discouragement. When we call on him, even when we feel like simply calling it a day, he hears us.

We can lead and love our families better when we remember he is *our* loving leader, a grace-giving heavenly Father, a God who is always there.

> Lord, help me open my heart to your presence in
>   all facets of my life.
> Fill me with love to pour out onto my family.

Susan Besze Wallace

1

Dawn

God Is with Us . . . in the Firsts

He is before all things, and in him all things hold
together.

Colossians 1:17

Baby's first Tuesday, first spit-up, first reaction to music, first time to meet grandparents . . . before you know it he or she has teeth, loses teeth, and bites down on life's disappointments.

Some of these firsts we pen in a baby book, while others are recognized only in a flash in our hearts, if at all, soon to be overlapped by the next experience.

God's presence in our lives can seem like that. Some days it's a more obvious, monumental experience or feeling. The Holy Spirit's leading in a moment or an encounter. An undeniable sense he is *there*.

Other times we are so caught up in the earthly manifestation of a new experience that we overlook God, his role in the situation, and the fact that he cares infinitely about each milestone.

Speak of newness in the Bible, and we immediately see Jesus in that scratchy manger, surrounded by adoring eyes. When the shepherds came to visit the newborn, "Mary treasured up all these things and pondered them in her heart" (Luke 2:19).

Such a peaceful image. I wonder about Mary's other firsts of mothering. Surely there were celebratory first steps for the newborn King. He learned to talk, to put on his own sandals. Were there uncertain firsts too? His first knock on the noggin? His first friend? His first hours away from Mom? Did Mary always acknowledge God in her child's firsts?

I once lost my toddler son in a nine-story hotel, thanks to slow feet and a quick elevator door. Ever since I have painfully related to Mary and Joseph becoming separated for the first time from their boy Jesus during a visit to Jerusalem. The search was anxious, and they found Jesus up to only good, listening to and answering questions from the elders. Though she didn't understand his reasons for lingering, Mary again "treasured all these things in her heart" (Luke 2:51).

That's what we're called to do as moms. When we take time to treasure things in our hearts, we can commit them there with the acknowledgment that we do not parent alone. God is in the firsts. When we celebrate even the tiniest feats, we get a glimpse of what it must be like for God to watch *us* grow . . . and stumble . . . and try . . . and stumble some more.

Firsts can test us and teach us, and they dawn anew with each child. Our kids are sort of like the miracles Jesus performed. His first was changing water into wine at a wedding. "What Jesus did here in Cana of Galilee was the first of the signs through which he revealed his glory; and his disciples believed in him" (John 2:11).

He went on to heal the blind and raise the dead, and none of the nearly three dozen miracles he performed after the wedding paled because it wasn't the first. God was fully invested in each, just as he's fully invested in each of our children. Even if you've seen multiple children head to some sort of school for the first time, God is equally present in each new sidewalk shuffle. He's always there to hold a mom's hand when her child lets it go. Just as he was the first time, and will be the next.

Even if having a child "the next time" is a complete surprise. So many firsts come without warning.

It was easy to recognize God in the "firsts" of my second son: cord wrapped around his neck and a crash C-section. It took a little longer to remember God's presence when I first saw alarming splotches over tiny white legs. I had to remember God made every inch of him, even those harmless birthmarks called "café au lait spots." We joked that God spilled coffee on Luke because they were playing so hard. To this day, my son plays and talks like a caffeinated kiddo.

Andrew, a fisherman, is considered Jesus's first disciple. He was the one who asked, "Here is a boy with five small barley loaves and two small fish, but how far will they go among so many?" (John 6:9). Oh, the first he was about to behold!

Even the special group of men who witnessed Jesus's teaching and miracles and persecution and death on the cross— even *they* sometimes forgot about the Lord being there in and over all the "firsts." They questioned. They feared. They felt excited, daunted, sometimes incapable, and usually awed.

Pretty much the definition of motherhood.

When we acknowledge that God is with us in the firsts, we invite him to celebrate with us. We thank him, we praise him, we ask him to continue helping us from one new thing to the next. The more we acknowledge him, the more we *will* acknowledge him.

And from that awareness, our relationship with God grows. The firsts will never stop.

There is so much I face for the first time, God!
Help me not to feel overwhelmed but excited at
all I'm experiencing.

The Pregnancy Test

Alexandra Kuykendall

"For I know the plans I have for you," declares the
LORD, "plans to prosper you and not to harm you,
plans to give you hope and a future."

Jeremiah 29:11

Hiding in the locked bathroom, I tore open the plastic package. I'd taken lots of pregnancy tests, but this one felt different.

In the past, I'd counted the days until it was test time, watching the calendar and then the clock, hopes high that those magic hormones would be present and strong enough to show positive. Most often, the tests were negative and my period came within hours or days, confirming my disappointment. But three times those magic double lines appeared, indicating a child was on the way.

Those three children were the audience I was now locking out of the bathroom.

I could hear them on the other side of the door, my eight-year-old practicing piano and my five-year-old chasing the toddler with a squirt gun. My husband Derek was working in the garage at the other end of the house, so the squeals were unlikely well supervised. But my nerves couldn't wait; a convenient time to spend five minutes alone never existed. So with the background noise of my life softened by the locked bathroom door, I took the test.

I immediately recognized the positive sign on the little white stick.

No. Not possible. This was not what we had planned. We were trying NOT to get pregnant. I started sweating. *How could I possibly take care of one more person? Wasn't the current chaos in my house evidence enough that I should not be trusted to supervise one more life?*

Derek. I needed him. I could hear squirt-gun girl on the other side of the bathroom door. "Genevieve," I said as I opened it a crack.

Splat. I was squirted in the face.

"Go get Daddy. Tell him I need him in here right now."

I used my sleeve to wipe water from my face. *Splat.* She got me again before running off.

I shut the door, smiling, but tears started to join the water already trickling down my cheeks. *How can I experience so many strongly opposing emotions at once?* Fear and dread combined with excitement and potential. *Derek's going to die.* I could hear Genevieve screaming through the house.

"Daddy! Mommy needs you!"

My mommy brain couldn't help but think she hadn't quite followed directions. I could have screamed for him from the other side of the house.

Derek, knowing the purpose of my secret bathroom mission, materialized quickly. I opened the door to find him with eyes wide, searching my face for a clue that his inkling might be correct. My laughing and crying grew stronger. He stepped into the bathroom, quickly shutting the door to keep out the hovering squirt-gun girl.

"What?" His eyes asked as much as his voice.

"It's positive," I answered.

We stood in the bathroom staring at each other. Confusion. Excitement. Fear. Surprise. After seconds that seemed like hours, Derek finally said, "This is great!" I could tell by his face that his words were genuine. He could tell by the look on mine that I wasn't feeling the same way.

"I'm just overwhelmed right now," I said through my tears. But we both knew Derek's reaction reflected a holy moment in the bathroom. Despite our best efforts to make life work according to our plans, God had intervened and created new life for our family. My fears of the unknown might hold me hostage for a while, but I knew God's hand was direct and I couldn't help but be in awe of that.

We didn't have much time for deep reflection, so we shared a few minutes more of laughing, crying, and general shock-related comments before we opened the bathroom door to face the mayhem. Another shot of water in my face greeted me as I exited the bathroom.

Back to my chaotic life, but with the quiet knowing that another baby was on its way to join our family, and this was God's plan.

Reflections

What's a situation that recently took me by surprise? Do I believe God when he says he has a plan to give me a hopeful future? Why or why not?

When the Third Is a First

Beverly Hudson, with Susan Besze Wallace

> They will not labor in vain,
>> nor will they bear children doomed to
>> misfortune;
> for they will be a people blessed by the LORD,
>> they and their descendants with them.
>
> Isaiah 65:23

I don't do my makeup until she's ready to crawl in my lap. We dab and fluff and pucker together. Her big smile at having her own brushes and empty jars fills my heart.

This is so new to me, raising a girl. My two sons preferred camouflage pajamas and taking G.I. Joe diving in the Igloo cooler. Bows and ruffles and pink now color our world.

I didn't expect this child. I didn't ever expect to see a baby weigh 1 pound, 12 ounces and cause an entire community to hold their breath as she fought to take hers. God knew this girl needed that community, and that she would need me, in a special way.

I have done this before, but it's a whole new ball game—make that a whole new dance party. I quit a job to give her my time. I am more mature, more focused. I have a few regrets about the way I handled the boys' early stages. I'm hoping to be more intentional with this little miracle, celebrating the snow showers of fruit puffs before I sweep them up. Twirling more often. Laughing more readily. Hugging harder. Hugging all of them harder.

As a woman, raising a girl means I am looking in the mirror more, and not just when primping. She will reflect much of what I show her. I want to help God fill her with strength and compassion. I want her to be so well acquainted with virtue that she won't shy away from it when she leaves this house.

I want her to know how special she is and how her stability comes from walking with God, not choosing a man.

I didn't know how to spend quality time with God when the boys were babies. I read to them, and I prayed with them. But I didn't know how to *be* with God, let alone pass that on to my sons. For me, it took years and crisis to make that happen, to make my day begin with God's name, to give potty training over to his control, and to feel my garden-dirt-splattered presence was perfect in his sight.

The miracle has her own little notebook and pencil. We journal together, her marks just scribbles but our words unmistakable. *God is our friend. He is right here. All the time.* I want her to feel him. I can help her to know him.

Maybe the tenderness I see in her isn't related to her gender, but to how I approach her. I have seen first steps and heard first words before, but each new life can be a rebirth for those who nurture that life.

It's not about getting through the day now. It's about loving her through the day, with the grace of God. I can give both of them no less than everything I have.

Reflections

Am I growing in my relationship with God? Whether it's a new day or a new child, am I gathering wisdom and grace to pass forward?

The Swaddling

Jane Hampton Cook

You hem me in behind and before,
and you lay your hand upon me.

Psalm 139:5

All the helping hands were gone.

My mother had cooked for us. Miracle of miracles, my father had changed my newborn son's diapers. My husband had taken time off work.

After three weeks, my parents returned to their home a thousand miles away, and my husband went back to work. He managed a large group of people in an intense environment and needed me to take night duty.

Also gone were the healing hands that had guided me throughout my pregnancy.

"See you in six weeks," my doctor had said, dismissing me from the hospital. I didn't realize how dependent I had become on her support through each stretch of pregnancy.

How I longed for a new cheerleader as I tried to comfort my inconsolable infant one lonely night. It was 1 a.m. He was well fed. I tried every comfort technique in the book—and video.

"Shhhh . . . shhhh," I whispered over and over into his ear, just as had been suggested. I rocked him, swung him back and forth, placed him on his side. Not even a pacifier would calm him.

Nothing worked.

Then I remembered one of the video's techniques: swaddling. Newborns have immature nervous systems. Their arms and legs flail when they are startled. Startling wakes them. Tightly wrapping an infant in a blanket can prevent both. I had given up swaddling Austin weeks earlier because he easily broke through my poor blanket-folding.

Remembering that Mary had wrapped Jesus in swaddling clothes, I figured it must be a good method. I found a blanket, swaddled him as tightly as I could, and placed him in the bassinet next to the sofa.

It worked. He was asleep. Thrilled but exhausted, I went to sleep too.

The next morning I grabbed a few quiet moments to myself. When my son was born I decided to read and meditate on Psalm 139, a beautiful passage showing God's intervention in each step of new life. My method was to copy one verse at a time in my journal and write my thoughts about it. Whenever I found time to read my Bible, I would shift my focus to the next verse.

Up next that morning: "You hem me in behind and before."

The timing was amazing. Hemming in. Swaddling. God swaddles *us* when we need his comfort and presence, as I did for my son the night before.

I reflected on how God swaddled me before my pregnancy. I had struggled for three years with infertility. He had "hemmed me in" before conception by leading me to a support group of women who were also facing infertility. The Lord "hemmed me in," guiding me to a new doctor who showed understanding and compassion and a willingness to take thoughtful steps when others pushed toward costly options.

During pregnancy he "hemmed me in" through doctors who wrote prescriptions for pregnancy's ailments. After

Austin was born, the Lord enveloped me in the care of my parents and husband.

And in the dark of night he reminded me of the swaddling technique to comfort my crying infant. From that moment, I looked at God's love and presence in a fresh way. I knew I could tap into his promise to be with me as a mom and provide wisdom and direction to help me adapt to the changing needs of my children.

When we are startled or upset, God swaddles us. His hands gently hold us and tuck us in when we need his presence the most, whether in the dark of night or the dawn of a new day.

My new cheerleader had been there all along.

Reflections

Do I sense God "swaddling" me during the uncertain firsts? When do I most need to feel his secure comfort in my life?

Proclaiming Our First Words

Caryn Rivadeneira

May these words of my mouth and this meditation of my heart
　　be pleasing in your sight,
LORD, my Rock and my Redeemer.

Psalm 19:14

As he led his Thomas train around the table, my two-year-
old son Henrik said, "He's gonna pick up more eggs."

I stopped pulling my own train, smiled at Henrik, and
asked him to repeat.

"He's gonna pick up more eggs," Henrik repeated dutifully,
pointing a pudgy finger toward the "eggs."

I crawled around the train table and kissed Henrik on his
head. My baby's first pronoun.

By age two, Henrik had already had his share of firsts:
teeth, steps, words, plane rides, attempts (though *only* attempts) at the potty—but the power of his first pronoun
caught me off guard.

I mean, nobody mentions this one in the baby books. There
was no blank for me to fill in. And yet, somehow, Henrik
using "he" properly left me a bit misty-eyed and amazed at
my little creature.

As a student in linguistics class in college, I learned about
the science of language development. But as I watched language develop in my firstborn son, it was all miracle to me, especially such language firsts as pronouns and past tense—the

sorts of things that require more than just understanding which combination of sounds represent which object.

As our children develop the intricacies and peculiarities of language, we catch our first glimpses into the way their minds work and process life. We learn that they really are listening, following what we say.

With each new word, with each conjugation, we hear the results of months and years of their brains chugging along, soaking up everything. Even as it seems every fiber in their body is focused on the tasks of eating and pooping, they grasp complex thoughts and then learn to proclaim them.

With the miracle of developing language, we witness another miracle. As we rejoice as our children's vocabularies increase—learning to form their own complex thoughts into complex sentences, learning to tell their own made-up stories—we discover yet another bit about the way God loves us.

In Psalm 19:14, David writes, "May these words of my mouth and this meditation of my heart be pleasing in your sight, LORD, my Rock and my Redeemer."

Before I had kids, I read this verse differently. I assumed it was all about making sure I didn't swear or say mean things. But being a mom and a writer, feeling the rush of hearing my toddler's first pronoun, I read this on a whole new level.

I think David understood the joy God takes in us as our language and our meditations develop, as we wrestle with the mysteries and complexities of our faith and begin to pronounce what we've learned from watching and listening to God.

While earlier in the psalm David writes of wanting to be blameless and free from sin's ruling power in his life, much of this particular psalm speaks of the truths David has learned about God and of the way creation proclaims God's glory.

So now when I read this passage, I have a new image: God sitting with me as I go through the regular stuff of life—pulling my little trains on a table, as it were—and smiling at me, crawling over to kiss my head, even, when he hears me utter a newly discovered word or a newly discovered truth about who he is and how he loves me.

Far from being a God who cares only that we "watch our mouths" (although, to be sure, he does care about this too), God is pleased when we discover him and when our mouths, along with all of creation, proclaim his glory in a new way. I love that.

Reflections

Which words of my mouth and meditations of my heart need to be more pleasing to God? Am I able to savor my children's firsts and let them show me more about myself?

Her Example

Ronica Stromberg

> When they had seen [baby Jesus], they spread the
> word concerning what had been told them about
> this child, and all who heard it were amazed at
> what the shepherds said to them. But Mary trea-
> sured up all these things and pondered them in her
> heart.
>
> Luke 2:17–19

It happened everywhere I went.

"Is your son walking yet? Mine did at ten months."

"Your son is still in diapers? Well, they say girls are easier to train. My daughter was dry by two."

"Have you tried _____? It's supposed to make your baby smarter."

My son Josiah was the oldest among the children of my friends and acquaintances but also the slowest. While younger babies crawled, he seemed content to lie on his back and meditate. While others pulled up on furniture, my son struggled to sit without toppling over. He was fourteen months old before he walked.

His pediatrician reassured me, "He's in the average range."

So why was I surrounded by so many mothers with above-average children? And why did they keep pointing out the differences?

When they asked about my son, I was truthful: "No, Josiah isn't doing that yet." After a while, I stopped these comparisons early by saying, "My son's slow at everything."

But then something startling happened. Josiah started talking. While the other children only cooed, he used full sentences and sang songs. He could recite the ABCs at eighteen months. He talked so much I put him in Mother's Day Out one day a week as a break.

When I picked up Josiah from the five-hour program, exhausted nursery workers would hand him over. One told me, "Usually at this age, kids don't say much. But you never have to wonder what Josiah's thinking. He'll tell you."

Another time a worker said, "You'll never guess what Josiah did today. We had the kids in their high chairs for snacks, and Josiah started singing 'Somewhere Over the Rainbow.' He even waved his arm like a cabaret singer. I've never seen anything like it."

I took Josiah to the pediatrician for his two-year checkup. The pediatrician wanted to check Josiah's eyesight, so I expected him to pull out the letter chart with the big E. Instead, he brought out simple pictures of everyday objects.

"Aren't you going to use the letter chart?" I asked.

"No," he said. "You can't count on children this age to know letters."

Josiah did, I knew, but I said nothing.

The pediatrician explained to Josiah he was going to hold up a picture for him to identify. He held up a picture of a moon. "What do you see?"

Josiah responded, "A crescent moon."

The pediatrician stopped, astonished, and put away his pictures. He remarked how verbally advanced Josiah was.

"He was slow at everything else," I reminded him.

"Sometimes children are that way because they're working on a different skill," he said. "He might have been working on language skills while other children were working on crawling."

As this discovery was made, I resisted the urge to trumpet it to other moms. I'd had enough of comparisons and felt no desire to diminish the accomplishments of other children. I found myself rewording the catchphrase "What would Jesus do?" to "What would Mary do?"

What would the mother of the only perfect son in the world say when other moms compared their children with hers? If a mom said, "My son took his first steps," would Mary respond, "Jesus walks on water"?

I don't think so.

I remember the amazement the shepherds shared at Jesus's birth and how Mary "treasured up all these things and pondered them in her heart" (Luke 2:19). The mother of the world's only perfect son had been humble.

Her example is one I want to emulate.

Reflections

Am I allowing my child to develop his or her own gifts and talents without comparing with others for my own affirmation? How can I parent humbly?

2

Matching Socks

God Is with Us . . . in the Mundane

And we know that in all things God works for the good of those who love him, who have been called according to his purpose.

Romans 8:28

We call them "God skies" in our family.

You know the ones: an early-morning or late-day canvas of impressive clouds through which sunlight streaks and is filtered in such a way that your eyes can't help but linger on the art of it all. I was proud of myself for labeling it for the kids. *See God's power, his beautiful creation?*

Then one day my middle son remarked, "There's no God in the sky on Tuesdays, Mom."

To be sure, it was a gray, flat, midweek morning of nothing significant. We were running to get groceries, only to return

31

to a messy house, mounting laundry, and the same boring lunch choices. Flat Tuesday, indeed.

When the hospital bracelet has long been removed and the monotony of motherhood settles deep, we can forget. Forget the magic of toes the size of peas and the delight of folding sweet-smelling miniature clothes. We refocus instead on the dirt those toes leave behind—and the actual peas that have rolled away and fossilized—and the need for the stain stick on those little clothes . . . again.

Life gets tedious; tedious is trying. If we're not careful, the repetitive tasks that fill our days can drain our spirits.

Hopefully my son's commentary was on the sky, not his mom.

In the Bible, it's easier to see God in parting seas and miraculous healings than in the long journeys, heart-hardening waiting, and daily grind of shepherding. But we know his purposes were at work there too.

On that flat Tuesday, I tugged my kids through the store parking lot, trying to move quickly to beat oncoming cars and whining. My son's comment echoed in my mind. As we climbed over a yellow curb cutout, I suddenly stopped, inspired.

"Jump off as high as you can when I count to three, okay?"

We were now superheroes. And it took fifteen minutes and two stops to watch some ants before we reached the store. The day hadn't changed, but I saw God in legs that could jump and in the smallest of his creatures. And I told my kids so.

Most of life is decidedly not like a trip to Disney World. It's more waiting in a hot queue than the rush of a ride. *But what do we do in the queue?* The idea here is not to compare our days, but to realize that if we are too busy grumbling, or so focused forward on the next holiday or family visit, we won't be able to serve and see God today in whatever numbing tasks lay before us. He's there.

And we are of value to God right now, in the plainness of today.

That means digging deep and doing what we do, "whatever you do . . . for the glory of God" (1 Cor. 10:31).

"Glory," one of the most common words in Scripture, is translated as "weight" in Hebrew. Even in lowly, repeated tasks like changing a diaper or scraping dried bananas off high chair straps, we can give God weight in the matter and realize both our children and the privilege of being a mom are gifts, manifestations of his goodness.

As John the Baptist said, "He must increase, but I must decrease" (John 3:30 KJV). Even in the little things, God can be big.

Glorified.

Perhaps we're all "God skies." Some days we toil in shadows. But with the right mind-set, we can always open up to the amazing light he offers.

Life can seem monotonous, God, but help me
remember only you last forever.

Remains of the Day

Sue Jeantheau

This is the day the LORD has made.
Let's rejoice and be glad today!
Psalm 118:24 GW

It seems like I just got dinner on the table.

Now, the dishes sit piled in the sink and the crumbs are piled on the kitchen floor.

It seems like the day just started too, but sunset's glow in the front hall tells me it's nearly over. The girls will need tucking in soon, and I wouldn't mind a tucking-in myself after another whirlwind day, the details of which have truly blown by me.

If it weren't for the crumbs.

The day's sprinkles and spills beckon the broom and dustpan. I had once considered this nightly ritual an exercise in spit and polish (either of which also could be on the floor on any given day). But over time, God has given me an opportunity to see him in that dust.

Tonight my dust pile included chocolate crumbs from my husband's birthday cake and grass clippings—a reminder of God's blessing of another year upon this man who provides for us in all he does, doting on his daughters and taking care of our home and yard. It also reminded me that even though I am now restricted to a gluten-free diet I can still share in the family's favorite celebratory, and flourless, cake.

Sand and wood chips indicate that some children had time outside, enjoying the late spring sun and the bounty of the backyard. Little flecks of color burst through. They are fallen chips of paint from the flowerpots of my daughter's end-of-year teacher gifts. A white twist tie stands out from the mix. *A twist tie? What does that go to?*

A lone popcorn kernel that didn't make it to puffiness brings me pause, as I think about how my big girl has grown old enough to make popcorn, and, more importantly, to invite her little sister to share in the bowl.

The word *dust*, I learned, has interesting roots. It means chestnut-brown or misty-gray. It shares the same root with the word *fury*, as in a brown, gray, raging dust storm. I'm pretty sure we had some of that kind of dust as well today. Our kitchen table is the place for all our meals, messy crafts, homework, and countless other activities. On occasion, confusion and turmoil live there too.

At the end of the day, the powdery gray dust of fury fades amidst the more colorful bits of sprinkled dust—the remains of a day that God chose to unfold just for us, a day in which we could rejoice and be glad in it and in him.

While it could be drudgery, the daily pickup of dirt has instead become a peaceful time of reflection, as I see not only snippets of life but ponder God's working through it. I marvel, humbled, and am ready to face another day tomorrow.

And find that white twist tie's home.

Reflections

Does taking care of my home lift my spirit or deflate it? What seemingly frustrating evidence of my day could actually bring about gratitude or joy?

Midnight Feeding

Karen Wilber

> At midnight I rise to give you thanks
> for your righteous laws.
>
> Psalm 119:62

Mmmm, sleep.

Encased in smooth sheets and soft pajamas, I rested my cheek on the cool side of the pillow. A ceiling fan swirled the night air, the only movement in the still, dark night.

At least that's how it was in theory.

In reality, I was up. Again.

I fumbled for the switch on the alarm to turn off that horrible siren until I realized that the noise was coming from my infant son. Remembering that he has no off switch, I lurched from my bed, banging my foot against the crib, to scoop him up and stagger toward the living room.

I craved sleep. I was so tired that when I was asleep, I dreamed about sleeping. I've never liked being woken up during the night, a fact my husband can attest to. Early in our marriage he would get the urge for a conversation, perhaps a little romance, or decide to search for something in his dresser . . . in the middle of the night.

Like a pink-pajama-clad Medusa, I would rise from my pillow, hissing, my hair splayed out in every direction, my eyes searching for a victim. I would freeze him with a stare and snarl some remark that would never come out of his daytime wife.

He learned never to wake me up.

My son became the only one who could rouse me without retribution. Upon successfully navigating the door frame that led to the living room, I would find the old rocking chair, bang my other foot against its wooden rocker, and slump down to nurse my son.

I loved him. I did not love being awake.

He got what he needed and I got back to . . . well, I didn't always get back to sleep. Sometimes the combination of loud wailing, sudden waking, hitting my head (elbow, knee, ankle) on some object, and twenty minutes of vapid staring into space while breastfeeding kept me up for another hour. It was a difficult arrangement.

One night, after I had finally been able to get to the 2 a.m. feeding without bodily injury, a thought crossed my mind. *Pray.* Pray for what? *Pray. This is a good time to pray.* Through the fog I remembered a prayer request from my professor. He had asked his students to pray for his wife, who was undergoing some treatments for illness. I thought I'd give it a shot. This would be the perfect time to pray: no phone interruptions, no television, and I couldn't see how messy the house was.

I was a captive in a rocking chair—every night.

I'd love to say those first 2 a.m. prayer sessions were filled with great spiritual meaning, but they were mostly mumblings and sleepy, half-formed thoughts. But I prayed. I prayed for my professor's wife. I prayed for my family. I prayed about my classwork and deadlines. Soon there was no end to what I brought before God in the middle of the night when it was just him and me and my nursing baby.

It was then that I really first felt the joy of motherhood.

The 2 a.m. feeding became my quiet time. I felt peaceful. I even began to look forward to that middle-of-the-night cry calling me to enter into uninterrupted prayer. Little did I know how short that season would be, for my son soon began to sleep through the night.

Though I loved the sleep, I regretted the loss. The 2 a.m. feeding that fed my son had also fed my soul.

Reflections

Do I confine my relationship with God to certain times of the day? Am I missing the beauty in the seemingly thankless moments?

Full

Nancy P. Mendez

So whether you eat or drink or whatever you do,
do it all for the glory of God.

1 Corinthians 10:31

Once again, my husband declined my dinner. He'd enjoyed another five-star lunch with his boss and some banking clients.

"I'm still stuffed," he said, eyeing my one-star menu of barbeque beef with macaroni and cheese. As my four-year-old son and I chewed our meal, my husband detailed his most recent feast.

"You should have seen this food, Nancy. Crab legs this long, dripping in butter," he said, his fingers delicately patting his lips and his eyes rolling back in culinary reverie. "And the desserts! You would have loved it."

The green-eyed gourmand in me had enough.

"Ya know what I had for lunch today? A corn dog and a juice box," I huffed.

"Nancy, when's the last time you were taken out for a meal like I had?" my husband asked.

Was that a proposal or was my jealousy his after-dinner drink? He seemed to be guzzling rather than sipping it . . . how gauche.

I glared at my fork laden with processed cheese. Since our move to Houston two years ago, our date-night punch card had gathered dust. Paying a babysitter was something we never had to do when we lived two blocks from my in-laws. Now three hundred miles from grandparents, the annual bank Christmas party was my one sparkly-earrings evening of the year.

Watching my son maneuver his miniature spoon, I recalled MOPS (Mothers of Preschoolers) meetings and the many mentor moms who had "been there, hated that." One especially droll dame recalled days she "dined" on the crusts of her toddler's peanut butter sandwiches while her husband entertained clients. I wasn't the first mom to suffer a replay of her husband's gourmet exploits, and I wouldn't be the last. The heartburn I felt was better known as envy.

I looked at my husband and considered our very different afternoons. My son and I had shared dogs and juice at the children's museum. On our way home, his big eyes shined in my rearview mirror as he announced, "I don't just like the children's museum. I loooooove it!" We had milked a fiberglass cow, filled our grocery baskets with plastic produce, and compared the viscosity of honey to maple syrup.

I put down my fork.

"How blessed am I to get to eat corn dogs with my son. So many moms would trade places with me in a minute to be with their kids as much as I'm with ours." One by one, the balloons at my pity party shriveled like sunken soufflés. "It must be hard to sit with your boss and make conversation all the time. I couldn't do what you do."

God had blessed my husband with the gift of gab and me with infinite patience—just what was needed for our very different lines of work. As my husband endured hours of meetings, commutes, and banal chitchat, I built Lego skyscrapers, played Candyland, and scraped Play-Doh from the carpet until my eyes crossed.

I'm sure we both felt like running for the door many days, but our jobs definitely had their perks. For my husband, it was a plate of crab legs followed by tiramisu on the bank's dime. For me, it was listening to my son chatter away between bites, just like his father.

Now I was the one daydreaming at our dinner table as I realized my heavenly Boss had also asked *me* to entertain a very important client today, one who enjoyed two-dollar corn dogs. I rejoiced that my hardworking husband relished his special meal. And the Lord added one more blessing to my helping of thankfulness: leftovers for dinner tomorrow. Maybe that will be the perfect occasion for those sparkly earrings.

Reflections

Do I hide or harbor resentment about the dailiness of my days? What is my idea of an ideal dinner, and has it changed since becoming a mother?

Potty-Time Ponderings

Kimberly Henderson

> The king [is] enthralled by your beauty;
> honor him, for he is your Lord.
>
> Psalm 45:11 TNIV

My potty-training tot sat smiling in front of me. Tiny feet dangled and kicked playfully as we waited for a little bathroom action.

I couldn't help but smile back at her. After months and months of resistance to anything related to using the potty, my youngest was finally getting the hang of the whole bathroom thing. The moment felt big. Important. My baby was growing up.

As we sat quietly smiling and staring at one another, I began to study her face, taking mental snapshots of some of my favorite things about her. Her beautiful hazel eyes sparkle with mischief and joy. Her itty-bitty nose and oh-so-squeezable cheeks cling to toddlerhood. Her sweet, tight-lipped smile always has me smooching.

I was overwhelmed by how much love I felt for her. I was completely enthralled with my daughter's beauty. Enthralled with her beauty . . . Psalm 45 came to mind.

God, is this truly how you think of me? Is this how you feel when you gaze upon me? Are you enthralled with my beauty?

I love my daughter right at the stage where she is. How I relish every new thing she learns. How I delight that she is not only learning to write letters and numbers, but that she actually *wants* to learn. I am in no rush for term papers. I don't need her doing math. I enjoy the right now.

I'm about to pee my pants because she's finally *not* peeing her pants.

The Lord was trying to speak to my heart right there in the middle of our guest bathroom. And I finally heard.

God loves me right where I am. No matter what stage I am in with my spiritual growth, he looks on me with love. He isn't mad at me because of what I just don't get yet. He does not have a constant frown etched on his face, frustrated with me because I am growing so slowly, because I still struggle with certain sins.

Yes, he is calling me to more. But he is still delighted with my efforts. His heart is full of joy as he watches me grow as his child. He isn't in a rush for me to master everything in his Word today. The Lord is pleased with every baby step I take toward him, even if I feel like I am still trying to get out of my spiritual diapers.

He looks at this daughter of his, enthralled with her beauty, and smiles.

How grateful I am to serve a God who loves me so unconditionally. His love fills me with the strength I need to press on each day.

And how tender he is to whisper of his love for me wherever I am, no matter what I am doing . . . even in the midst of potty training.

Reflections

How can I tune in better to what God is trying to share with me? What "noise" in my life might be preventing that?

The Red Plate Reminder

Alicia Bruxvoort

Therefore the Lord himself will give you a sign:
The virgin will conceive and give birth to a son,
and will call him Immanuel [God is with us].

Isaiah 7:14

When my first daughter was in preschool, she came home one afternoon with a pressing question.

"Mom, what does Jesus like to eat?"

Distracted by a pile of supper dishes and a screaming baby in the infant swing, I answered pithily, "He probably loves fruit. After all, that's what he planted in the Garden of Eden." Satisfied with my shallow reply, Lizzy nodded her delicate head of blonde curls and ran out the door to join her big brother in the sandbox.

I didn't think again about my five-year-old's odd question until early the next morning.

After an endless night of pacing the floor with a colicky baby, I followed the aroma of freshly brewed coffee to the kitchen. I was exhausted and grumpy, overwhelmed with the thought of facing another round of diapers, dishes, and discipline. The day ahead loomed as colossal as the mountain of dirty laundry awaiting me in the basement. The realization that my three little ones would soon be awake fueled my funk.

I looked around my quiet kitchen and wished for a friend to share my angst.

Then I spotted it: a curious splash of red on the edge of our battered kitchen table. I rubbed my eyes, flipped on the light, and marveled at the stirring sight.

Set elegantly at the head of our old wooden table was a red china plate dotted with a clump of purple grapes and a shiny green apple. Next to the humble spread of fruit lay a cheap white paper napkin with a simple misspelled message scribbled in sloppy crayon letters: "Welkum Jesus."

Unexpectedly, my tired eyes teemed with tears. My wish had been granted.

I was not alone.

I slumped into a sticky chair near the crimson plate and echoed my little girl's invitation. *Please, Jesus, would you help me through this day?*

In the hours that followed, the laundry pile didn't miraculously shrink, nor did my fussy baby suddenly adopt an amicable attitude. But something inside me shifted. The plate perched at the edge of the table reminded me that I have a friend who understands.

Thirteen years of dirty diapers and dirty laundry have taught me to appreciate a Savior who dwells in the midst of my ordinary and in the midst of my mess. When I am weary, he shares his strength. When I'm discouraged, he offers hope. And when I'm frazzled, he gives peace.

These days, our kitchen scarcely contains enough space for our growing family of seven. But whenever we cram all fourteen legs beneath that old wooden table and settle in for the mayhem we call mealtime, I serve our food on bright red plates: just a simple reminder of the welcomed Guest who lives among us.

Reflections

How can my kitchen table better reflect God's presence in my family's life?

The Little Things

Jennifer Grant

> And he said: "Truly I tell you, unless you change
> and become like little children, you will never
> enter the kingdom of heaven."
>
> Matthew 18:3

There are times when reading Jesus's words about becoming "like little children" might make you laugh. Laugh darkly, that is.

Reflect on that verse while your kids bicker about who gets to use the tiny Lego light saber and you might find yourself asking, "Become like children? Really, Jesus?"

Consider it in the thick of potty training your child while clutching sticker charts and an unopened package of Thomas the Tank Engine underwear, and you might pray, "Become like little children? Really, Jesus? You want me to be exasperatingly stubborn and have no regard for personal hygiene?"

Or when you've set your child on the bottom stair to consider important truths such as "We don't hit" or "We don't throw food," you wonder if Jesus could have meant what he said. "Become like little children? Really, Jesus? You mean, should a spoonful of peas offend me, I should fling it across the room?"

Sometimes we'd be tempted to fast-forward over these intense early years if we could.

But even on good days, we work to move our children away from childhood. We want to help them grow and mature. The future is ever on our minds. That's just good parenting, right?

While we are nursing our babies, for instance, we think ahead to how to wean them. When they stack three blocks, we run our fingers down lists to see whether they are on track developmentally. As soon as they crawl, we pull them to their feet.

We're always pushing our children ahead on an unending march toward independence.

But then there's Jesus, telling us adults to move in the other direction and to "change and become like little children" if we want to enter his kingdom.

What in the name of Barney and Baby Bop could he mean?

Maybe his words have something to do with the way children are present. Unlike adults, little children don't divide their attention between multiple tasks and worries. They linger in the moments of their lives, whether those moments are delightful or disappointing or utterly simple.

They are real, present, and aware.

It seems only natural to children to stop what they are doing and watch a red-winged blackbird bob on a tree branch. It's only right to lick sticky palms, savoring the sweetness, after eating a peach. Puddles are for jumping in, bubbles are for popping, and when music makes them happy, there's no reason not to get up and dance.

Adults are too often distracted, self-conscious, and disconnected. Perhaps in failing to see, smell, taste, and hear signs of God's goodness and grace around us, we lose touch with him. Maybe when Jesus says that we must become "like little children," it's one way he invites us to connect with him in an authentic and openhearted way.

Like a child.

And sometimes we do. Sometimes we step away from our worries and fears. Sometimes we unplug from laptops and cell phones. We let ourselves get carried away and do things that aren't very rational or grown-up.

We lie in the grass and watch the clouds.

Or raise our hands high in the air just because we feel grateful and happy.

Or we dance in the rain.

And, in these moments, as fleeting as they may be, we get a glimpse of heaven and we remember that our loving God is always with us.

Even on the bad days.

Reflections

What, to me, are the best parts of being a child? How can I reflect a more childlike approach to my days and my faith?

3

Duty Calls

God Is with Us . . . in Our Sacrifices

Walk in the way of love, just as Christ loved us
and gave himself up for us as a fragrant offering
and sacrifice to God.

Ephesians 5:2

There we sat, way before cell phones or other electronic distractions. Sweat beaded on my forehead from my fever and saliva accumulated in my mouth as I tried to prevent swallowing on a sandpaper throat. Miserable, yet oddly content, I hoped for a prescription to stretch out the evening.

My biannual bronchitis was never a picnic, but being one-on-one with my mom was its own sweet affair. That time together is truly among my fondest childhood memories. Care, compassion, conversation. Of course, at the time I wasn't thinking about how deep my mom had to dig to spend the evening and part of her teacher paycheck at the after-hours clinic, again.

She showed me sacrifice long before I knew the word.

I think of her and our hours together every time I take my kids to the doctor. I hope they see comfort in my eyes, not a frustrated, calendar-centric woman thrown off course.

I know God is there. I've learned to invite him to hold my hand while I hold theirs.

As mothers, we sacrifice from the moment the stick shows a line. We change our eating habits and become inhabited. Paul wrote in Romans 12:1, "I urge you, brothers and sisters, in view of God's mercy, to offer your bodies as a living sacrifice, holy and pleasing to God—this is your true and proper worship."

There's not much choice when you're pregnant. And much of mothering out of the womb requires sacrificing different pieces of yourself—your time, your sense of order, your priorities.

But there's *requiring*, and there's *offering*. And that's where God is in our sacrifice.

Abraham offered his son Isaac to God when he asked (see Genesis 22). A poor widow offered all the money she had to live on to the temple treasury (see Mark 12:41–44). Paul offered his health, safety, and freedom for the cause of Christ (see 2 Cor. 11:23–28).

None of those acts was done in disgust. All were done for God.

When God offered his son Jesus to the world, it was to give us a chance to repent and dedicate our lives to him (see John 3:16). Sacrifice is a symbol of holiness, not a punishment. We draw nearer to the character of Christ when we're offering.

Sometimes I think the big ones are easier. I spent nine days in the hospital with a sick seven-month-old, never venturing out for fresh air once. It was a privilege to be the person my little man needed. So why is it harder to stomach sacrifice when it just involves a child's stomach lurching all night? Or simply a change in our plans?

We are still whom they need. We are still the woman God wants to love on that child, in that way, at this time.

Could it be perhaps that there are so . . . many . . . times?

We have love. We don't always have the sleep, patience, money, or answers mothering seems to require. So we offer what we have, in love. We ask God for the rest (and the rest). And because "Love bears all things, believes all things, hopes all things, endures all things" (1 Cor. 13:7 ESV), we can keep offering.

"If anyone serves, they should do so with the strength God provides, so that in all things God may be praised through Jesus Christ" (1 Pet. 4:11).

When we sacrifice, something is being done *for* us, not *to* us. We're being given a chance to grow closer to the holiness of God.

> Lord, when I huff down a dark hallway, feeling
> the sting of sacrifice, meet me there.
> Help me to find joy in the offering.

Someone Else's Timetable

Helen Lee

This is how we know what love is: Jesus Christ laid down his life for us. And we ought to lay down our lives for our brothers and sisters.

1 John 3:16

I could hear the phone ringing, but it took me a while to find it, buried in the piles of half-folded laundry on my bed. No doubt my three-year-old son had assumed that "hiding the handset" was the new game of the day. I threw aside socks and underwear as I answered, fully expecting to hear my husband's voice on the other end of the line.

"Hello, may I speak with Helen Lee?"

I was jolted by the professional tone in an unfamiliar woman's voice. She was an executive at the well-known Christian publishing company where I used to work, and although it had been many years since I'd last been an employee there, she had tracked me down to ask if I was interested in working with her, in a new position that sounded exciting and just right for me.

My mind whirled with the possibilities. I'd been wanting to work part-time, to start exercising my gifts and abilities in some tangible way again. Perhaps this was the chance I'd been looking for. But then I looked over at my son, who was creating textile sculptures out of towels and T-shirts. I tried to sound casual and asked, "Could part of this job be done from the home? Is telecommuting an option?"

The executive paused. She replied, now with an apologetic tone, and explained that the position would require someone onsite full-time. I thanked her for thinking of me, politely declined the offer, then lay on my bed next to my son and cried.

I felt certain I was called to spend this season of my life primarily caring for him and his infant brother, who was asleep in the next room. But even so, the reality of making this choice meant I was often leaving behind something that I deeply wanted. Some days I would give up something seemingly small and mundane, such as sleep. Other days I was giving up a potential dream job.

The life of a mother is filled with moments, small and large, of laying down her life for her children.

Making sacrifices for our kids is not something that receives accolades in our culture. Society celebrates celebrity moms who seem to have and do it all, conveniently forgetting that these women have enough hired help to run a small city, far from the reality of most moms' daily lives. The world sees and envies these moms—and if I'm honest, I do too, at times. I may love seeing the occasional kid-crafted textile sculpture but would gladly sacrifice those moments if someone whisked away all my laundry!

But God sees you, and me, and he smiles each time we put aside our own desires to serve and care for our little ones. No matter what sacrifices I am making in my life now, I know they pale in comparison to what Christ has already sacrificed for me.

Although I feel that I will forever be living my life on someone else's timetable, in fact I am living out God's timetable for me, on a heavenly schedule I may never understand to the fullest but that promises to be the best plan possible for my life.

Six years have passed since the phone call that drove me to tears. But recently, the same executive who called that day has come into my life again, now as a member of my writer's group, someone with whom I will be able to create and craft words in community. I never could have predicted that one day our lives would circle back to one another and we would in fact get to work together in a tangible way.

But God knew.

Reflections

What are the toughest sacrifices mothering has demanded of me? Would I act differently if I lived mindful that God sees my little offerings as well as the large ones?

This Is My ~~Job~~ Privilege

Jennifer Sammons

For it has been granted to you on behalf of Christ
not only to believe in him, but also to suffer for
him.

Philippians 1:29

I was almost nine months pregnant and had my fifteen-month-old girl on my hip as I waddled back into the living room. I knew what had happened from halfway down the hall. I could smell it.

My three-year-old son was going through the granddaddy of gross phases. He was struggling with potty training and had recently started digging his poop out of his underwear and smearing it on whatever he could find. This time it was the wall, the floor, the little rails between my kitchen chairs, and all over his whole body, including his face.

I had just quit my job to stay home full-time, a gut-wrenching decision. In that moment, as I discovered the collage of nastiness, I questioned my new career change beyond measure. I was angry with my son and with my life.

Worst of all, I could see no end in sight. This was it: poop, crying kids, and exhaustion.

I was the one crying as I scrubbed with a rag and a bucket of soapy water, trying to disinfect everything. Through my tears, I mumbled angrily to God, "Really, *this* is my job?" The hardest thing to get clean was my son. I didn't know if any amount of soap was going to get his fingernails completely clean and every time I smelled his little hands I got more discouraged.

It shocked my son that his mommy was crying. He was worried about me. My angry heart softened as I hugged him out of the tub and tried to have a rational conversation with him.

As I held him, I marveled that neither this, nor any other yucky sacrifice I would endure as a mom, could make me stop loving him. I tried my best to offer up this sacrifice to God as a prayer.

For in that moment, I understood what it meant to be a child of God: unconditional love.

It was an eye-opening glimpse of the overarching love God must feel for me and all his children. "See what great love the Father has lavished on us, that we should be called children of God! And that is what we are!" (1 John 3:1).

I now seek God the most in these really trying and sacrificial moments of motherhood. I often ask for divine intervention, offering up sacrifices as a prayer, many times while I'm enduring them. Doesn't matter if it's a real biggie, like a medical crisis, or something that seems big, like making it through the supermarket with a toddler mid-tantrum.

By praying while I experience these inevitable joys of motherhood, I hope to imitate the example set by the apostle Paul. "Now I rejoice in my sufferings for your sake, and in my flesh I am filling up what is lacking in Christ's afflictions for the sake of his body, that is, the church" (Col. 1:24 ESV). While I'm no Paul and there is nothing lacking in Christ's redemption, it's in these moments that I'm given an earthly opportunity to share in Christ's suffering. In the process, I feel I'm growing closer to Christ.

Yes, even through the hard-to-stomach moments.

There is a hidden joy in the duties that I do not choose, but which choose me. They give me the opportunity to better love my children. And they unite me more closely to our Lord.

I'm getting much more than I'm giving.

Reflections

Can I give God my words in the midst of giving so much to and for my kids? What would I say to him about today's sacrifices?

The Night Shift

Suanne Camfield

This is the confidence we have in approaching
God: that if we ask anything according to his will,
he hears us. And if we know that he hears us—
whatever we ask—we know that we have what we
asked of him.

1 John 5:14–15

It was, by far, my favorite way to come home: my husband and I in the front seat, fresh off a date night.

The kids were tucked behind us in their car seats—snuggled in their pj's, bathed by someone other than me, and, most importantly, drifting off to sleep.

Pulling into the driveway, we were moments away from being home free. No diaper changes, no drawn-out bedtime routines, no power struggles, no "One more drink!" or "Tell me a story!" Just a short walk up the stairs, a careful closing of the door, then quiet.

Quiet that we—the parents of two toddlers just fifteen months apart—desperately needed.

Ah, but my daughter was going through a *phase*. Somewhere just shy of her third birthday, Sadie had decided sleep was overrated and reverted to the pattern of a newborn, waking every three hours to scream her head off.

For the better part of a year, we had tried everything, and I mean *everything*, to settle her down. Nothing seemed to work. Night after night, we'd take turns shuffling down the hall (sometimes gently, sometimes forcefully), but we always failed to make the quiet last. We were exasperated and completely exhausted.

So on this night, with the promise of sleep dangling euphorically over our heads, you can imagine our frustration when we laid Sadie in bed and the screaming commenced. For two hours we did our best, but by midnight the battle escalated to such heights my body quaked with anger.

When my husband slipped back into bed next to me, again, and the crying began, again, I gritted my teeth. "That's it!" I said. "I've had it!"

I threw off the covers with a grunt and stomped down the hall toward her room, ready for a fight of monumental proportions. I was not backing down.

But when I got to the doorway of her room, I froze. Then I melted.

There, sitting in her toddler bed, the red patchwork quilt that accompanied her home from the hospital draped toward the floor, Sadie was sitting upright with her knees pulled to her chest, her elbows on her knees, her forehead resting on her fingertips.

Between ragged breaths and choking sobs, I could hear her plea. "Please, Jesus, I need my mommy."

My little girl was doing the very thing I had taught her to do a hundred times before. "When you need something, sweetie," I'd say, "just ask Jesus. You can ask him for anything and he'll give you whatever you need."

Remorse replaced my anger and I walked slowly, gently, across the room. I crawled in bed next to her. I wiped her tears, stroked her hair, and kissed her cheek. I cried tears of my own and asked God to forgive me.

Somewhere between searching for the "right" parenting technique and holding my ground, in the midst of all the noise and in my sheer exhaustion, I had lost track of the idea that what my daughter most needed was me. Despite my impatience and anger, God still chose me to be the answer to her prayers.

Her breathing gradually slowed and her body relaxed. "It's okay," I whispered. "Mommy's here."

She was asleep in an instant. And although I can't be sure, I have a feeling she was resting in the confidence that God hears her prayers and provides for her needs, even in the form of tired, cranky parents.

Reflections

When I feel I can't dig any deeper, can I hand God the shovel?

Waiting for Normal

Letitia Suk

Give thanks in all circumstances; for this is God's
will for you in Christ Jesus.

1 Thessalonians 5:18

My neighbors led a "normal life," or so it seemed.
Dad walked home from the train at the same time
every night. They could always say, "Dinner is at six." I en-
visioned their Saturdays as a blend of quickly done chores
followed by entertaining outings.

I was so envious.

Our family's life was not "normal." Sometimes the dad in
our house, my husband, didn't finish work in time for dinner,
or maybe even until after the kids were in bed. Our Saturdays
were spent waiting for Dad to come home from work before
the fun began. Definitely not normal, in my mind at least.

Not content just to notice our abnormality, I mentioned it,
complained about it, resisted it, and mostly waited for it to
be over so we could get around to having that elusive normal
family life. For years.

I decided to just push the pause button on family life. *Why
bother with a real dinner?* Dad wasn't going to be home anyway, so why not open another box of macaroni and cheese?
*Sure you can watch another movie. We can stretch your bed-
time again.* No order, no routine, except on the nights Dad
was home. After all, we weren't a normal family.

I'm not sure what incident toppled the fragile stack of *whatever* building blocks I'd built our family life with. Maybe we ran out of paper plates or pizza coupons. More likely, an insight of truth and conviction made its way into my nagging heart. For our family to thrive during this season, I could no longer wait for my husband's hours to change. The change needed to come in me.

I thought I was sacrificing normal. But I didn't realize God had given us a different normal. My husband may not have been there, but God was always in our home, waiting on me to wise up as I waited for some standard of living I had created. It was time to redefine normal.

My husband was the first to benefit from my change of heart. I realized how difficult it was for him to try to get out of the office to be with us and then be greeted with grumbling. I apologized for grousing about long hours and thanked him for providing for our family. He was surprised but relieved to hear my support of his hours as well as his employment.

Without making a speech about it, I started serving dinner at about the same time each day with real food, cloth napkins, and a couple of candles. The kids especially liked the candles, appreciating that I was honoring them, not just company. Bath time and books were a little harder to get in without an extra set of hands, but the payoff of established rituals offered structure that worked for all of us.

Day to day, my new normal was more satisfying than negativity and exhaustion from staying up too late and arguing with the kids about things I'd let them get away with.

I still got the I'll-be-late calls and the kids still had meltdowns, but we got through it. It helped to remember that my husband and I were on the same team.

My husband's hours eventually changed, and he was home more often. It seemed like just a minute before our four children grew up and left home one by one, and we had to learn to redefine normal all over again.

I am the only guest for dinner some evenings now. Occasionally I enjoy a slice of pizza on a paper plate, but I remember to first light a candle and put on some music. Now that I am no longer waiting for normal, it is always right at hand.

Reflections

Am I waiting for a circumstance in my life to change instead of living fully now? How could I better embrace my new normal as a mom?

Playground Rules

Nicole Russell

> Stop storing up treasures for yourselves on earth,
> where moths and rust destroy and thieves break
> in and steal. Instead, store up treasures for your-
> selves in heaven, where moths and rust don't
> destroy and thieves don't break in and steal. Your
> heart will be where your treasure is.
>
> Matthew 6:19–21 GW

I noticed the playground right when we moved in.

It was small. Old. Plastic, and covered in a layer of dirt. It sat smack-dab in front of my kitchen window.

"At least Beckett can play there," my husband said, referring to our son. I scowled. It was an effort to redeem himself for picking an apartment two times smaller than I'd specified in an area where petty crime, unkempt yards, and noisy neighbors abounded.

I had left the comforts of my family and home state to support my husband's new job and pursuit of further education. I also assumed we were heading to the East Coast to embrace an upwardly mobile lifestyle. After renting a few months we'd move into a nice home in scenic Virginia; on the weekends we'd hire a babysitter and venture into Washington to dine on tasty cuisine.

As I struggled to fit appliances in my tiny kitchen, I glanced out the window at the multicolored playground. I was, to say the least, disappointed.

A few months later, a series of financial setbacks meant our temporary eight-hundred-square-foot living space would be our home for another two years. I became angry and disillusioned with God. How could he allow me to bring my second child home to a cramped, dingy space that made me feel humiliated?

We had to change everything not only to become financially sound again, but just to make ends meet. I resented this sacrifice; I let my husband and a few close friends see my bitterness. I had created a concrete cocoon of expectations about my life and felt eager to see them met.

God began to chip away at them.

The spacious house I imagined became a memory. We had to store most of our belongings, including a different season's wardrobe. We nixed eating out—unless we had a coupon— nearly altogether.

We removed our cable and cut our grocery bill. A taxing purchase was a new pair of shoes for my husband, who walked to the bus and took that to work, since we had only one car. It wasn't uncommon to go a week teetering on the edge of overdraft fees with ten dollars in the bank.

Entertainment consisted of walking to 7-Eleven to split a Slurpee then going home so our son could play on that playground—oblivious that anything might be missing. Creative experiences and learning opportunities came in all forms and at little or no cost, a lesson I hope to remember on this parenting journey.

Gradually, God took my scripted, preconceived notions about the "good life" and morphed them into his own act. I learned paying bills and being responsible with money was worth more than showing friends a nice, large home (even when our newborn daughter had to share a bedroom with her big brother). Date night could be just as romantic by swapping kids with another family and eating somewhere cheap. Family fun didn't have to be a day at a theme park, but going to a free festival and then eating dinner at Costco for six dollars.

In a few months, God not only changed my perspective on needs versus wants, but as my wants dissipated and my needs were satisfied, I appreciated the transition instead of feeling embarrassed and sorry for myself.

The last summer there, I set my lawn chair in front of our apartment, directly across from the playground, and soaked in the sun while my kids giggled and slid down the dusty slide. God forced me to lay down the happiness I sought in exchange for an entirely different kind. He illuminated what was always in front of me: the playground wasn't a sign of oppression but of opportunity. Giving up what I wanted didn't mean going without what I truly needed.

Reflections

What do I need to work on in my relationship with money?
What do I truly treasure?

4

Holding Hands

God Is with Us . . . in Our Marriages

> Be devoted to one another in love. Honor one an-
> other above yourselves. Never be lacking in zeal,
> but keep your spiritual fervor, serving the Lord.
>
> Romans 12:10–11

We stand on opposite sides of the bed after dark, quietly attacking the laundry heap together. At least I attack. He sort of watches TV and moves things around.

Should I be flattered or frustrated he just flopped my running shorts on my nine-year-old's pile? It's a certainty that every child will end up with someone else's something. In my male-only household, a bra is the only thing sure to get to the right spot when my husband is folding.

But he *is* folding.

He doesn't see me silently trying to will him to stop needlessly triple-creasing underwear. Then he picks up mine, and smiles.

Oh this man.

Oh this marriage.

I smile too.

What an amazing thing that God took his two most similar creations and designed them to couple, forever, knowing how truly different men and women would ultimately be.

God is here in my quest to find some sleep underneath all the tightie whities. He is helping me view this mate of mine with softness, not superiority.

As a younger mom of even younger children, I would have tossed judgment and my-way insistence on that pile. An unpleasant stew of sleep deprivation and sarcasm stunk up many precious days of my marriage. I knew it even as the words spewed out of my mouth.

In an era in which entire TV shows are dedicated to the trappings of weddings, it's easy to forget *God designed marriage*. He orchestrated that "a man leaves his father and mother and is united to his wife, and they become one flesh" (Gen. 2:24). When we remember that God is behind our coupling—that he has plans for it—I think we can more readily find him in it.

I used to see my marriage like a rowboat tied to a dock. Depending on the weather, or my mood, I'd float (or thrash) to and from the thing, the man, who gave me security. Luckily the rope never broke. *Was God that twine?*

Years lived, and two babies mourned, my vision for marriage has changed. My husband can't be my dock. We need to unite in the boat to brave whatever current comes. We need to paddle together—though not necessarily alike. God is the only true port in any storm.

In his book *Sacred Marriage*, Gary Thomas asks a potentially life-changing question: *What if God designed marriage to make us holy instead of happy?*

The Bible shows just that: couples persevering, often falling flat, growing closer to their Lord. Zacharias and Elizabeth stayed together when her barrenness would have been acceptable grounds for parting (see Luke 1). Mary and Joseph had to trust each other deeply to make the journeys and the decisions that came with raising Jesus. The lesser known story of Hosea and Gomer is one of unimaginable forgiveness and unconditional love (see Hosea 1). The union of Abraham and Sarah is marked by struggles we can all relate to: challenging moves, questioning God's timing, jealousy, and submission (see Gen. 12–22).

"Happy" though some may have been in certain moments, "holy" is what saw them through.

Parenting can strain us as couples. It can also strengthen us. God wants us to cling to one another and to his promises to make us better, together. He is there, in the late-night words we wish we could take back. In the words we can still say. In the spontaneous kisses. In the back rubs and the backseat whining. In the knowing glances over little achievements. In the disappointments, the date nights, and all those decisions. And even in the folding of underwear.

> *Help me open this gift of marriage each day,*
> *Lord, with renewed joy and with thanksgiving*
> *for what you have in store for us.*

One Love, Many Movies

Kathi Lipp

> Be completely humble and gentle; be patient, bearing with one another in love.
>
> Ephesians 4:2

W ill Smith? Come on, you like Will Smith, right?" Roger is almost at the point of begging, right there in the middle of Best Buy.

"Yes, but I like the *Hitch* Will Smith, not the *Independence Day* Will Smith. Okay. Clearly we aren't finding any dramas. How about a comedy? Oooohhhh, this looks good!" I feel a surge of hope.

Roger crinkles up his nose, "That's not a comedy, that's a chick-flick. Get it if you want. I'm sticking with Will Smith."

After fifteen minutes of pouring over DVDs and taking his and her movies up to the counter, I look at Roger and say, "Well, it's official. Again. We're movie incompatible."

This issue of "marital incompatibility" is not a new discovery in my marriage, but it's never more evident than when we are trying to find a movie to watch together. Or when we are seasoning our food. Roger likes his food *muy caliente*. I'm a salt-and-pepper girl.

In fact, there are a lot of areas in our marriage where we are downright misfits. When we were first married, these differences frustrated me all the time. How could I be with someone who likes to spend a weekend sitting in the woods swatting away bugs or spends his vacations standing in line at the Hottest Place on Earth. Later, when it came to parenting our blended brood, his idea of a severe punishment was to send his daughter to her room (you know, the one with the iPod, cell phone, and enough tween novels to stock your local library), while my kids felt grateful if there was bread and water served with their no-technology lockdowns.

During the first year of our marriage, I would often have pangs of loneliness. Roger was always working or serving at church, and during his downtime his way of relaxing was a good *Star Trek* episode.

I was frustrated with him, and I was frustrated with God. Why didn't I have a man who wanted to spend time with me? If we couldn't agree on how to spend time together, how were we supposed to make a marriage work?

It took me a couple of years to realize that in that time of dating before we got married, I never sensed the loneliness because I didn't care what activity we were doing. Camping? Sure! Let me grab my s'mores stick. A Star Wars marathon? I'll bring the popcorn. When we were dating I probably would have agreed to bear wrestling as long as I got to hang out with Roger.

Somehow, once we were married, I expected that Roger would want to do the stuff I liked, because we were now, well, married. And yes, sometimes, Roger will watch a Renee Zellweger movie, but only because he loves me.

When I was a single mom, I trusted God to meet my emotional needs through his Word and his people. When did I stop fully relying on him to meet my needs and put that responsibility squarely on my husband's shoulders?

God has provided women through church, MOPS, and Bible studies who share my love of the sacred and the silly. These are women who hold me accountable in my life—and hold a great Saturday afternoon giggle session. With them in my life, why was I mad at Roger for not wanting to watch *Pride and Prejudice* with me?

God provides other healthy relationships, so my husband doesn't have the pressure of being everything to me all the time. He doesn't always have to be my confidant, confessor, and cheerleader. We can still love each other and look forward to lots of anniversaries.

When I've nurtured the other bonds in my life, Roger has the freedom to play his most important role: husband.

Reflections

Where do I see God's presence in my marriage? How can I prevent little frustrations from obscuring the bigger gift of my relationship?

When You Just Keep Blowing It

Ann Voskamp

[Love] does not dishonor others, it is not self-
seeking, it is not easily angered, it keeps no record
of wrongs. . . . It always protects, always trusts,
always hopes, always perseveres.

1 Corinthians 13:5, 7

When I'm still brushing my teeth on a Sunday and the
kids, all ironed and parted and combed and waiting,
scuffle loudly at the door, he pokes his head in, near the mirror, and he says it quietly.

That we are almost too late for church now anyway, that
it's nearly 10:30 already and there isn't much point as we'll
be at least fifteen minutes late now.

I huff ridiculous, snap sharp and say, fine then, you can
all stay at home, the whole lot of you. But I've got to go, my
name typed out neat for this week's nursery supervisor, and
I slam the door on my way out.

The children all scatter.

I drive to church alone and wildly sad.

The nursery is empty. The ache in me is emptier.

Sometimes the most impossible person to live with is
yourself.

In the babyless nursery, I turn up the volume knob to hear
the pastor. It's the next chapter in our study of 1 Peter. I rock.
A baby, then two, collect on my lap. I rock. I can hear the

pastor reading this week's text: "In a similar way, you wives must submit yourselves to your husbands."

I heave a sigh, close my eyes. Rock. One baby tugs at my beaded bracelet. I feel the Spirit's tug. I'm undone.

I don't know how I'll go home.

He already has lunch on the table when I walk in awkward and slow. I don't say anything. I'm always surprised at how hard it is to open your mouth and admit you're a fool.

I go to change out of pinching black shoes. He slips in, soundless, and sits at the end of the bed, one foot resting easy across the other. I find Birkenstocks. And I sit down beside him, uncomfortable, staring straight out the window. Two starlings flap about in the top of the cherry trees.

Why do I blow everything, again and again? *Will I ever be who I already am in Christ?*

My chest hurts. I know what I have to say.

I turn toward him, and my throat's raw and sore. Our eyes meet, and we search for a flicker. And in that moment, the Spirit flame descends and I feel its tug. It comes unexpectedly, a relief that he feels it too: we both smile sheepishly.

Our eyes light.

And our lips both offer it in the same moment, and we speak in one tongue, speaking one word: "Sorry."

We hold hands when we pray at lunch. Through this season of Easter we've been reading, slowly and repeatedly and deliberately, from Acts, and today it's the seventh chapter. My husband the farmer reads, "You stiff-necked people! Your hearts and ears are still uncircumcised. You are just like your ancestors: You always resist the Holy Spirit!" (v. 51).

I close my eyes, bow my head.

Grace rocks, comforts the impossible.

He lays his hand on my shoulder. We pray. We submit to one another. We wash the dishes together.

After the last plate's stacked, I go for a walk. My littlest one comes with, and she does a dandelion run. She laughs as the dog chases her, and they spin across the globed fields.

I watch and I ache. Why do I obliviously slam the holy moments with frustration?

When she moves and breathes I watch it—how dandelions take to the sky.

I feel that pang in my chest again. I will blow it but to repent and return, turn to the cross. To not resist the turning. To submit to the Spirit blowing in again and again.

No one ever blows it so badly that the Spirit can't still blow in.

And no wind ever blows so hard that it doesn't carry hope, that it doesn't blow in blessings too.

To kneel and receive both, the impossible made possible by grace.

Reflections

How am I handling the times when I disappoint myself, my husband, and my God? What keeps me from forgiving others more readily?

Showing Up

Mary Ellen Blatchford

Dear friends, since God so loved us, we also ought
to love one another. No one has ever seen God;
but if we love one another, God lives in us and his
love is made complete in us.

1 John 4:11–12

My husband heard me crying in the shower.

I often went there to let go of my tears because it was the only place in our home that offered me quiet solace.

We were raising four young children, two of whom had been diagnosed with a rare genetic disorder that doctors claimed would progressively worsen over time and cause premature death. Some days it all just became too much. The shower was my place to release the heaviness I carried.

He heard me crying.

I opened my eyes and saw he had climbed in to be with me. He held me close and quietly said, "I love you. I do not know what will happen to our children, but I will go through it with you. I promise."

My tears did not stop. We both knew he could not diminish my pain. In fact, he had his own to face. But he was willing to enter the darkness with me, and that brought a quiet relief.

My beloved husband John died unexpectedly and suddenly ten years later. Facing life as a single mom, and still managing the illnesses of our children, I often thought about that moment in the shower. His love lived on after his death.

Those words he whispered gave me an enduring strength. I was blessed with a husband who taught me the importance of "showing up."

God did not convey that suffering would always ease or that pain would disappear. Just that his presence could offer us hope in the midst of anguish.

God never leaves us alone. He's there in the shower tears, or the closet meltdown, or the sunshine of a beautiful day. God shone through John often. He taught me how to "show up," especially in marriage, without trying to micromanage, fix, or worry a situation to death. Just be there.

It has been many years since that moment when water and love poured out in unison. I don't recall all the details that took me there that day. But what remains crystal clear is the gentleness of John's words, his comforting touch, and most of all his willingness to step toward me in my time of sorrow.

We never know how many tomorrows we have left. But in our marriages we can all choose to let God work through our willing hands, feet, and loving arms.

And we can all love someone in a single moment in a way that will echo in their hearts forever.

Reflections

How am I doing at truly treasuring my spouse and our life together? Do I "show up" when crisis arises or shut down?

Empty Places

Ashley Larkin

Satisfy us in the morning with your unfailing love,
that we may sing for joy and be glad all our
days.

Psalm 90:14

I sat on the corduroy couch with my husband in the steel-blue den of our first house. Neither of us spoke. The room felt like rain.

I loved this man. I resented this man. Our two daughters slept down the hall.

I knew Michael's words were true, but accepting them felt like clothing myself and our marriage in defeat. How could one created to be my partner, my complement, my love, say these things?

"I cannot satisfy you. I will never be able to give you what you need," he'd said.

The words slugged me in the gut, and then the dull pound of accusations began. *He could satisfy you if you were less complicated, less demanding. If you built him up more with your words, if you weren't so busy caring for the kids, if you gave him more attention, then he would be able to give you what you need.*

Part of me wanted to walk out the door as I had during our first big fight our first year of marriage. Garbage can in hand, barefoot, I had felt momentarily powerful when the door slammed behind me. I knew I'd stunned my husband. Now he was sorry.

Then I had looked down at myself, surprised I was capable of giving up on him. I walked back through the door to Michael, who wore a wounded look upon his face.

This time, as we sat on opposite ends of the couch, I thought of our girls and our love for them. The love that opened our hearts each day to pour out again. A love that woke every morning to make breakfast, change diapers, read *Goodnight Moon* and *Guess How Much I Love You*, teach about God, encourage new adventures, bandage elbows, cradle, hold.

I always thought if I tried hard enough I'd never truly disappoint my kids. But in spite of best efforts, we disappointed. Fell short. Hurt feelings. Lost tempers. My husband and I were a good parenting partnership, but we saw that no matter the depths of our care or effort, we could never satisfy our children's deepest needs alone.

A dim light of understanding began to glow.

I wanted my husband to love me perfectly, understand me completely. I would hold hopes for what he would say, and then be crushed when he didn't get it.

But the wounded places in me were mine. Empty wells of longing and worth-seeking that I tried to fill, or have my husband fill, just leaked. I covered ugly messes of self-doubt with patched tarps of effort, and they blew away.

This time, I saw the cry in my heart as one for God. I felt it. As I sat in pain that night, I remembered times God came when I simply asked and admitted that I could not do it all alone.

Please fill my empty pools. Please cover me.

Both captives on the couch needed releasing. Michael was right. He could never satisfy me. He could never give what I needed in the deepest, hungriest places. He could never fully soothe me with enough words to cover insecure flesh. I was like our children—taking and still wanting and needing. I was that baby bird, mouth open—always screeching for more to feed the ache in my belly.

I looked away from the wall and into Michael's eyes. "You are right," I said at last.

When I stopped expecting my husband to perform himself into my grace, I started partnering with God. I began to give the acceptance in my marriage that I'd hoped to receive. I could delight in this man and see God at work in us. A prison door had cracked open.

In admitting my weakness, I could receive God's strength. And I could receive Michael as my loving husband.

Reflections

How have my expectations of my husband changed since we were dating? Have I changed my expectations of myself? Are God's goals for my marriage different from mine?

Hope

Michelle Rahn, with Susan Besze Wallace

> Let the morning bring me word of your unfailing
> love,
>> for I have put my trust in you.
> Show me the way I should go,
>> for to you I entrust my life.
>
> Psalm 143:8

"Mom, I thought you said I didn't have to go to church today . . . that I could sleep in!"

The backseat whining from the younger of my two girls coincided with a sisterly punch.

"God knows our hearts, and I just know that he *and* I desire you to be with our family today."

"Then how come Daddy isn't coming with us? How come God lets *his* heart stay at home?"

There it was again. The question that made me so weary I quickly tried to avert it with a new subject. I asked it too, every Sunday. My husband and I had been round and round, with his bottom-line reasoning being, "I never missed church as a kid, all the way through high school. I just don't want to go now. God understands, so why don't you?" I emphasized the importance of our kids seeing him there. Apparently I was a wonderful example, and that was enough.

I herded little dresses through the parking lot with hands and words, delivered them, and plopped into the pew closest to the door.

I love it here.

I love to sing.

I . . . I am surrounded by couples, flanked only by my purse and my Bible.

I wonder what people think when they see me alone.

I met my husband in the sixth grade. I loved him still. I just wanted him to want God. I wasn't feeling superior, or even angry, just a bit sad in the blur of young motherhood.

I prayed, "God help me to love him and see him through your eyes." It helped. But other thoughts would creep in.

How can I teach Sunday school if I can't teach my husband to come to church?

Because he wasn't mine to teach.

After years of this lonely but ultimately uplifting Sunday morning shuffle, my mother died. I sang for her memorial service. I felt the presence of Jesus that day so real and strong—he was the one singing. It was then that I knew I wanted more of Christ in my life and began to pursue not just church, but a relationship with him.

My prayers for my husband intensified, but my burden decreased. I had to grow to know God personally before I could truly see that my yearning would not change anything. Only God could do that.

We all are initially shown love and exposed to faith in different ways—if at all. I respected the man in my life. And I waited. On him, and on God.

I let love take over.

Personally, I use music to praise God and find perspective through all life's frustrating moments. Thank goodness— thank God—that he knew I'd need volume and melody for all sorts of circumstances. As Romans 8:28 reminds us, "In all things God works for the good of those who love him."

So my husband had one journey to take, and I had another. Sitting between my purse and my Bible wasn't my idea of the perfect arrangement.

But now I know I was never, ever alone in a pew.

Reflections

Do I want to change my husband? How can I better see my mate through God's eyes and love him as such?

5

In the Dark

God Is with Us . . . and in Control

But I will sing of your strength,
  in the morning I will sing of your love;
for you are my fortress,
  my refuge in times of trouble.

Psalm 59:16

The chorus of gasps surprised me. I was watching him, too, my young son atop a high spiral playground pole, about to spin his way down.

I realized my mom friends weren't about to let their kids go there. I had been at first impressed with my little guy's confidence. Then suddenly, *I* had none. Peer pressure had me ready to shout a cease-and-desist order, when he twirled down—in delight, and in one piece.

On the playground, I never knew exactly: *How close did I need to be?*

The first broken bones in our three-boy family would come many years later, when a rack of balls fell on a collarbone during a supervised *story time*. And then another when a different son pulled a bench down on his foot while calmly getting up from *dinner*. Neither was playground bravado, and I was superclose both times.

Is there ever "close enough"?

Control is a confusing issue for moms. We are supposed to determine limits, bedtimes, and portions, and teach character, academics, and hygiene. But even while holding tightly to the things we manage, we need to acknowledge the Great Manager and remember he is always there and in ultimate control.

God is in control even in the dark moments in rocking chairs and on bathroom floors and, yes, in playground mulch. And in even darker moments in exam rooms and funeral homes. We grapple with reacting in crisis, soothing our children, changing unpleasant realities, and maybe even who to blame. Recognizing God's presence in the decidedly undramatic times helps us cling to God when life hits those inevitable spiritual potholes. "The Lord upholds all who fall and lifts up all who are bowed down" (Ps. 145:14).

People have always faced the question of how big God is in their own lives. Moses wasn't sure he had what it took to lead his people to the Promised Land (see Exod. 3:11). David's people faced a standoff with the Philistines, but only this eighth-born boy had the courage—or perhaps the faith—to face the imposing Goliath (see 1 Sam. 17). Job's wealth, children, and physical health were taken in Satan's attempt to get him to curse God.

"The Lord said, 'Everything under heaven belongs to me'" (Job 41:11). And Job, asking many, many questions, hung on:

"I know that you can do all things; no purpose of yours can be thwarted" (Job 42:2).

Some of us moms are more controlling than others, but I think having children makes it even harder for all of us to live blind to what life will hold. We want so much for our little people—health, joy, security—that when those plans are upended, even a slight bend in the road can feel like a severe and painful detour.

God doesn't promise that all the roads will be pleasant to walk, or that we'll understand the "map." He does promise that we'll never walk alone. "With God all things are possible" (Matt. 19:26), and often that thing is simply enduring with faith.

God desires that a woman be "clothed with strength and dignity, and [laugh] without fear of the future" (Prov. 31:25 NLT). Laughing doesn't come easy in darkness. But we can't live in fear of life's spirals, playground or otherwise. We do our best to keep our kids safe. I did everything I could to help my daughter survive in the womb. It didn't work.

So yes, we can be only so close.

Thankfully God stands in the gap, and stands ready to love us through anything.

> *I want you to be in charge God, but I also want what I want!*
> *Help me hear your voice and feel your strength.*

O, Retch That I Am . . .

Amy Henry

Therefore do not worry about tomorrow, for
tomorrow will worry about itself. Each day has
enough trouble of its own.

Matthew 6:34

I hate throwing up.

I really hate it when my kids throw up.

I even hate anything remotely related to throwing up, including but not limited to small children choking on frozen raspberries, retching noises made in jest, and the smell of Lysol.

It all started the time my seven-month-old daughter, Anna, and her three older siblings got a stomach bug. It was a terrible flu that seemed never to end, with Anna throwing up twenty-five times before I stopped counting. For a control-freak mother who hates vomit of any kind, it was a nightmare.

What was worse was that this week of sickness got stuck in my brain. From then on, every nighttime sound, every cough, every green look sent me into a panic. Once I was so convinced that the kids were coming down with something that I rushed into my son's room in the middle of the night, grabbed him out of bed, ran down the hall, flung up the toilet seat, and held his head over the bowl. Meanwhile he woke up, perfectly healthy, cast me a wild look, and began to howl.

But as much as we'd like to avoid it altogether, mamas know: throw up happens. Sometimes in the most inconvenient places. Sometimes at the most inconvenient times. Sometimes both simultaneously.

So, over the years, I learned that we could avoid throwing up if we just followed two simple rules: (1) never see people, and (2) stop living. At times it feels a small price to pay for health, as does living with hand sanitizer in every car and purse, insisting on clean hands after every dangerous germ-catching foray into public places, and avoiding crowds at holidays. Other times it felt like I might be a bit nuts. But the fear of two-week-long flu bugs going through the family fires up every OCD tendency in me, making no amount of effort in securing the perfect, hermetically sealed environment too much.

My fear of throwing up is more than just hating buckets and Lysol, though. It reveals a hole in my faith that isn't easy to admit. Because although I can control my children's schooling, their nutrition, their bedtimes, their friend choices, their hairstyles, their extracurricular activities, their nap schedules, and their amount of screen time, sickness reminds me that my illusions of control are just that, and despite all my carefully orchestrated precautions, all my hypervigilance, and all the hand washing, God is actually the one calling the shots.

Jesus said, "Sufficient for the day is its own trouble." Which is great if you're a relaxed sort, but if you're control . . . uh, challenged, it is as hard to swallow as one of those huge nasty prenatal vitamins. I know because I've been trying to do so since my first baby arrived almost eighteen years ago. I can honestly say it's only become modestly easier to accept as time goes by. Control is something I still keep a fingernail-only hold on, despite knowing full well that doing so is as fruitless as trying to potty train a three-month-old.

The famous hymn "Day by Day" says, "Day by day, and with each passing moment, strength I find to meet my trials here." Day by day isn't something control-freak moms normally do well. We're more in the "scope out the next six months and make sure everything is lined up just so" camp. But that leaves out that enigmatic element called faith, the knowledge that God will be there, giving us just what we need, just when we need it.

Which—when the kids are throwing up—is stat.

Reflections

What in mothering do I find hardest to give over to God's control? What would happen if I did?

There in the Raging

Amy Parham

My frame was not hidden from you
   when I was made in the secret place,
   when I was woven together in the depths of the
     earth.
Your eyes saw my unformed body;
   all the days ordained for me were written in
     your book
   before one of them came to be.

Psalm 139:15–16

Three boys in six years. Not sit-in-the-corner-and-play-quietly boys. Loud, rowdy, destroy-everything-in-sight was more common in my gene pool. My eldest's baby days were vivid, the second child's details a little fuzzy. By the time the third came along, I was a functioning zombie.

Some days, I blamed the chaos for my not seeing the signs. Some days, I thought if I hadn't been so busy and had played with him more, nothing would have been wrong. If I had held him longer, he might have been . . . normal. The if-onlys drove me to a pity party faster than Mario Andretti could take a lap at the Indy 500. I blamed myself, circumstances, and eventually God for the nightmare that I began to live when my youngest son Rhett was diagnosed with autism.

We all have dreams for our children both near and far: happy school days, high school success, college, marriage, grandbabies. Those imaginings quickly slipped away when I realized that with autism there was no cure and no guarantees.

I felt I was having a funeral for my dreams for my child, with no one to mourn with. He may never have a best friend or go to normal classes at school. He may never even hug me or express love unsolicited. He would hit. He would scream. He would climb out onto the roof, unbeknownst to me.

My family *knew* he would outgrow it. They couldn't fathom that a disability affecting 1 in 150 kids could have touched our family. I couldn't understand why God would let this happen. I had been in the ministry, after all.

I had shouting matches with God, telling him in no uncertain terms that he needed to fix Rhett. He had gotten me into this mess, so he needed to get me out of it. I raged. Told him I wasn't going to quit praying until Rhett was 100 percent healed. If I allowed myself to love and accept Rhett with his disability—if I relaxed—I was accepting there was no hope for normalcy. That was my quest: normal.

One day, while driving and having my daily shouting match with God, I heard a still, small voice in my heart. It wasn't audible, of course, but a clear knowing—a calm in my tornado of confusion and frustration, powerful enough to stop me in my tracks.

You are not perfect and I love you. Why does Rhett have to be perfect for you to love him?

I knew I'd be forever changed. All I needed was to quit trying to change Rhett and just love him. In doing that, I took the burden off me and truly put it on God. He'd been there in my raging, and when I was ready to hear it, he gave me a peace that had escaped me for years. The verse "Cast all your anxiety on him because he cares for you" (1 Pet. 5:7) entered my life that day.

I don't know what the future holds for Rhett. I do know that when I released him to God, I happened on several wonderful therapies that improved his behavior and ability to learn dramatically. He continues to make progress.

But it doesn't matter. Wherever he is, and whatever the future brings, I'm going to love him like God loves us. Completely.

Reflections

How am I doing at balancing my responsibility to take care of my child with God's ultimate control over my child's physical health and development?

Shelter in the Storm

Cindy Dagnan

But I trust in you, LORD: . . . My times are in your hands.

Psalm 31:14–15

It's just a sock. Tiny and pink, wreathed in lace. But I remembered opening it at the baby shower, and later, sliding it over an impossibly small foot. When the car wash vacuum inhaled it before I could save it, I melted down.

Another memory, another loss, another reminder of how little control I have.

It had been just a few days since an F-5 tornado packing 200 mph winds destroyed one-third of our hometown in Joplin, Missouri. It was only a few years ago that another tornado had sucked up our own house with the force and noise of a freight train, taking our possessions and memories with it, as my husband used his body to shield me and our four girls.

This time we weathered the storm in a church basement, five blocks away. My husband, the police chief for the county seat, trudged for nearly eight days through rubble and heartbreak. The mother whose baby was snatched from her, as the winds pried open the arms that tried to hold on. The father whose son, hours graduated from high school, was sucked through the sun roof as his father held on with everything he had. The daddy who sheltered two children as Home Depot

94

collapsed around them, leaving a mother behind with unimaginable holes in her heart.

I could only listen, take my husband a few supplies, and work a predawn shift registering law enforcement and National Guard dispatched to help. I could not stop my maternal tendency toward morbid questions. *What if that were me? Could I survive? How would I go on?* In hushed tones on the playground, and as we volunteered around town, we questioned it all. We questioned ourselves. There were fissures in our souls.

Two things I know to be true. I learn them all over again, as all of us mothers do whenever anything shakes our security. One, I cannot always protect my children. I will not always be around when they skin knees, fall off bicycles, or experience a broken heart. I must entrust them to God while teaching them to rely on him.

My four blessings are not really mine. They are the Lord's, and for this season he has given them into my care. In a way I cannot fathom, he loves them even more than I do. He will make decisions regarding all our lives that I do not always understand and may not always like.

Two, because we live in a fallen and sinful world, tragedy can strike. God does not promise us protection or divine intervention from every hurt, however much I wish it so. He only promises that he is there, the God of all Comfort, to hold us, to restore that which the locusts have eaten, to cause good to grow from that which makes us utterly broken.

There were too many funerals. It continued to rain for a week after the tornado, and lightning struck two officers. Does heaven weep with us?

We must decide in advance of the tornadoes of our lives—spiritual and physical—that we believe in God's goodness despite every feeling to the contrary. We choose to trust. It is imperative that I teach my kids to do the same.

Though we love our children boundlessly and would surrender our lives for them, we must leave them a legacy of faith. A rock-solid foundation that will not move, even if everything around them gives way.

Reflections

When crisis hits, what does my reaction say to my children? Do unthinkable tragedies challenge my faith in God's goodness?

When the Formula Fails

Carey Haivala

> He fell with his face to the ground and prayed,
> "My Father, if it is possible, may this cup be taken
> from me. Yet not as I will, but as you will."
>
> Matthew 26:39

The sheets twisted around my body. A shallow night's sleep spent in answerless frustration.

The alarm forced my dry eyes open, but troubled thoughts still spun: *How is Heidi?*

An ache settled into my heart.

Why does God let babies live for a few weeks then die just when we begin to love them?

Miscarriage seems a term too clinical to describe the crush it inflicted on my sweet sister-in-law.

My faith stung like a hard slap.

Tears fell as I let myself remember. Nine years ago, it was me. My babies on the ultrasound screen with no heartbeats. Twins. Five months of hope and joyful anticipation, erased in an instant.

"We have a problem. Turn off your video camera," the doctor told my husband.

My exposed midriff bulging, I lay on his cold table and wept.

My heart screamed. *What? It can't be true! We prayed. We believed. We trusted.*

Just like Heidi.

At five weeks, an ultrasound revealed she had two gestational sacs. We prayed and believed.

At six weeks, the sacs where the babies' hearts should have beaten . . . were empty.

The way I read it, the formula for answered prayer is clearly laid out in Scripture: thanksgiving + faith + repentance + persistence = granted request. Throw in some praise and humility and it's foolproof. *Right?* No. The equation doesn't always work.

I sat up in bed, still wrestling with questions. *How can we continue to believe and pray the same way?* My wavering faith made me feel guilty.

The pain in my shoulders traveled up my neck. The long night's battle still clanged in my spirit.

I never questioned if God was really able. It was more *Why wasn't he willing?*

I looked in the bathroom mirror and wondered if Jesus always got his prayers answered the way he wanted.

Almost always.

Jesus was in the garden the night before he died . . . praying. He was "sorrowful and deeply distressed."

He implemented the formula. He humbled himself. Asked his friends to pray. Had faith. He even one-upped the formula. He sweated blood, pleading, "Father, if it is possible, let this cup pass from me."

Then, Jesus did something remarkable. He said, "Nevertheless not as I will, but as you will."

Jesus realized that God has higher purposes.

As I padded downstairs, my son Daniel's sweet morning face met me in the hall.

"Mommy, can I please have a cookie?"

I secretly thought a good cookie might make us all feel better.

"No, honey. Not for breakfast."

Then it hit me. I had just rejected a request that seemed rational to Daniel. Not because of the way he asked, but for my own good reasons that were invisible to him.

He cried.

I scooped him up and leaned against the wall. We mourned for all of our denied petitions. Maybe our hardship is to complete character in us, or to help someone else.

Maybe we won't ever know. But we can trust the divine Decision Maker. Jesus did. It propelled him to the cross. God's purpose for "no" was our eternity in heaven.

As I poured cereal into Daniel's bowl, my eyes lighted on the cookie jar. I smiled, knowing I would grant his humble request right after breakfast.

When we crunched our cookies, I thought about Heidi. I prayed her next request would end the same: with sweet desire completely fulfilled and perfectly timed.

Reflections

Do I believe in a "formula" for meriting God's blessings or answered prayers? What concern can I resolve to hand over to his control today?

Hands

Michele Cushatt

> If I rise on the wings of the dawn,
>   if I settle on the far side of the sea,
> even there your hand will guide me,
>   your right hand will hold me fast.
>
> Psalm 139:9–10

In a sea of forty thousand strangers, my four-year-old son disappeared. One moment my hand swallowed his. The next, he was gone, melted into a pressing crowd.

I'd crossed the finish line moments before, out of breath and drenched in sweat. My husband and three young boys had waited over an hour for me at the end of the race, along with a stadium filled with other spectators.

It was my first 10K, a huge physical and emotional challenge, and one that I'd spent months training for. My well-worn tennis shoes crossed the finish line in sixty-two minutes, and within moments my husband and boys surrounded me with smiles and cheers. In an instant, fatigue and sore muscles disappeared in light of their proud faces.

My husband kissed my cheek, while the youngest pressed against my leg, as usual. He didn't like sharing attention with anyone else. And so he pushed closer and closer, determined to get in on the action.

In a second, he was gone. The crowd engulfed us all. When it parted enough for us to regroup, only four remained. The fifth and smallest family member was nowhere to be found.

Panic replaced elation. "Jacob!" I yelled, frantic. I scoured the crowd, seeking a four-year-old in an ocean of big and tall. Impossible.

Father God, please! Bring my baby back to me!

In the end, he was gone no more than fifteen minutes. Not nearly enough time to do a load of laundry or feed a fussy toddler, but to me, an eternity. We found him fifty feet away, hovering next to some bleachers, looking small but far less panicked than us. I ran to him, wrapped him in my arms, and whispered "I love you" again and again. Then I pulled back, put both hands on either side of his sweet face, and looked him square in the eye.

"You can't run away from Mommy ever again. You scared me. I didn't know where you were!" He acquiesced, nodding, noting my tears but unable to comprehend how his little adventure could cause his mother such grief.

"Yes, Mommy," he promised.

In time I'd learn it was a promise he couldn't keep.

He never again disappeared among thousands. But I've lost track of how many times I've panicked as I've watched the son I birthed slowly disappear into the man he will one day become. I've experienced the anxiety of knowing he was outside the reach of my protective arm the first full day of preschool. Later, as he grew, I watched him choose to do the opposite of what I'd taught him, tempted by outside influences. I lifted my desperate plea up to heaven.

Father, bring my baby back to me!

The moment I became a mother, I became the protector of my children. However, as time has passed, I've learned how very little control I truly have. My babies have been entrusted to me for a time, but ultimately they're not mine. A day will come when I'll need to let them go.

But just as my heavenly Father has guided me through my life, I can trust he will guide my children in theirs. I still have parenting to do, lessons to teach, and love to give. But when the world crowds in and I fear I'll lose them, I can either panic or trust.

Panic will rob both of us of life.

But trusting in a God who sees will help us both to truly live. I may be their mother, but God's the one who will lead them through the crowd and safely home.

Reflections

Have I lost something, or someone, that I need to trust God to nurture or restore? How am I doing at treasuring the young days of our family, as opposed to enduring them?

6

Girl Power

God Is with Us . . .in Our Friendships

Help carry each other's burdens. In this way you
will follow Christ's teachings.

Galatians 6:2 GW

Imagine a friend who never condemns, just asks questions.
She loves in spite of the fear of being judged or rejected.
She loves with all that love demands. She's never jealous. She
loves even the unlovable.

Particularly the unlovable.

Change the "she" to "he," and you have Jesus, the perfect
model for friendship. He even loves kids. Your kids, no matter what they do.

Friendships forged during the demanding phase of young
motherhood can last. It's a time in life that finds us growing,

learning—and needing. Bonding on that journey can sow seeds of trust and bring great joy.

But it's also a time that can usher in great insecurity, unearth old wounds, and show us where our own upbringing fell short.

Either way, God shows up.

His Word is ripe with instruction on productive friendships, and his world is full of women who can bless each other, if given the chance. Or the time of day.

I have many friends I wish I'd never had to meet. The girls in the grief group who lost babies like I did. The friend I met at the mall when I knew not a soul in town and asked desperately where she bought her kids' shoes. The friend who took care of my father-in-law and his heart in the ER one morning.

She's forever a part of *my* heart now, and most of my days.

Proverbs 17:17 tells us, "A friend loves at all times, and a brother is born for a time of adversity," and sure enough, many of my sisters were born *in* adversity. Isn't that what motherhood is so often—challenges to meet?

There are plenty of women I didn't meet. I was too absorbed in what I needed to make it through the day. Absorbed by the quest to have more children. Just absorbed, period. It's easy to become an island when you have small children.

But God calls us to build bridges.

"We encourage you, brothers and sisters, to instruct those who are not living right, cheer up those who are discouraged, help the weak, and be patient with everyone" (1 Thess. 5:14 GW).

Sometimes, of course, we are the ones who are discouraged. But bridges are rarely one-way. And God is there, paving the way between women who need him.

When you look at each woman you meet as someone God has put before you, it changes how you view friendship.

Whatever circle she's in, or season you are in, God wants us to live and serve in community. Seeing God's hand in our connections with other women can help us look beyond self, and be the kind of friend we want to have.

We're told clearly that sacrificial love is what we are called to. "Greater love has no one than this: to lay down one's life for one's friends" (John 15:13).

Many days we more accurately reflect David, in the Psalms, alternating between declaring our wretchedness, being honest with our shortcomings, and then suddenly ticking off our good deeds and our justification for . . . so many things. People are flawed. And friendships will be too. Some friends are the hands and feet of Jesus, that bridge to a better self. Others show us a path on which we can ditch faith for more earthly pursuits.

Who we surround ourselves with is our choice. God wants us to recognize his abiding presence in all our friendships. They are gifts our Creator gives us, precious mirrors we can use to see ourselves more clearly. What are you reflecting?

Lord help me to see in this busy season the
women you want me to love.
Help me look beyond myself to love fully and
laugh heartily.

Walking Alone for a While

Elizabeth Esther

Do not conform to the pattern of this world, but
be transformed by the renewing of your mind.
Then you will be able to test and approve what
God's will is—his good, pleasing and perfect will.

Romans 12:2

I was a young married mama, pregnant with my first baby
at age twenty-one. Even though I was happy, there were
times when being a young mama was lonely and disconcert-
ing. None of my friends were having babies, and even strangers often commented on how I was "throwing my life away"
or "missing important opportunities."

I'll never forget going into the bank one day and the teller
realizing that she and I were the same age. She leaned over
the counter and whispered: "Don't you feel like you're missing out on life?"

How could I be missing out on life? I was *creating* life!
And yet professors, friends, and even some family members
kept repeating those ideas to me. I remember breaking down
in tears after a friend warned me that I was in danger of becoming a boring Christian housewife who did nothing more
with her life than pump out babies and cook meals for her
husband. I felt so discouraged.

But that's also when I started learning my first lesson of
motherhood: giving others' opinions and comments too
much value would be detrimental to myself, my child, and

my relationship with God. God had blessed me with the priceless gift of a baby. I was not about to cheapen that gift by bemoaning my supposedly doomed "opportunities" and "wasted life." Instead, I decided to realign my priorities.

I had unwittingly placed a greater emphasis on having friends, pleasing my friends, following my friends, and doing what my friends did rather than following God and doing what he asked of me. Becoming a mother was a new direction for my life, and for a time it meant I didn't have a bunch of like-minded friends. But I was convinced that the gift and calling of motherhood was a great privilege. I wanted to live worthy of that calling, even if it meant I had to walk alone.

I didn't walk alone for long. I learned to speak cheerfully and happily about my new role as a mother. I quit apologizing for being "just" a mom. This was my way of honoring God and the gift of the beautiful daughter he'd given me. And as I did this, I found new, supportive, faith-centered friendships. Instead of friendships that were centered on just having fun or achieving personal fulfillment, these friendships were centered on a common goal: bringing glory to God through our vocation as mothers.

What this meant for me was that instead of seeing daily mothering tasks as mundane drudgery, I began to offer them as a holy sacrifice. Each small task could be rendered as a gift of love, an act of service. Indeed, each time I changed a diaper, made a meal, or swept the floor I was offering my worship to God. I learned to focus my daily life as worship to God, and then any friends who came along were happy bonuses to the joy God had already given me.

But even as these friendships have grown and flourished, I'm still learning how to listen to the still, small voice of the Holy Spirit. There are so many opinions, ideas, child-rearing philosophies, and popular parenting trends inside the Christian world that I have found cultivating a prayerful, Spirit-led conscience a vital necessity.

It's easy to jump on a bandwagon or rally behind some parenting ideology. But ultimately, honoring the Lord is my highest priority. Someday, perhaps, my children will see that. By God's grace, one day they'll call me blessed.

Reflections

How can I honor God in making and maintaining friendships? Do I believe he'd give me the strength to walk alone for a while if necessary?

A Balm to the Soul

Lori Wurth

> So encourage each other and build each other up,
> just as you are already doing.
>
> 1 Thessalonians 5:11 NLT

I wanted a friend, but not as much as I wanted to get rid of the ache and the anger.

It is hard enough to endure the roller coaster of infertility. Shots are routine. Modesty becomes a thing of the past. Hope is something you fight for.

But when hope and modern medicine unite in new life and you believe, truly believe for twenty weeks that you are worthy to create and sustain new life, the end of that life cuts so deeply you stop being able to share with God.

Water breaks, placenta disintegrates, and so does your faith.

In the weeks after our son Daniel was delivered stillborn, my husband threw himself into work and projects around the home to manage his grief. We talked some, but my needs were just too much for him.

We had recently moved to a new city, so in desperation I called our new church and they sent me Karen, someone they called a "trained listener," to help me process this enormous sadness. I was pretty nervous that first day she showed up at my house. What if she didn't get it? What if she didn't get *me*? What if I didn't like her? What if she didn't like *me*? It felt darn risky.

As we sat on the living room couch that first meeting, she won me over quickly. She'd been there and personally understood my pain and anger. I have never cried so much in my life as during those months following Daniel's birth and death. Her tears joined my tears each time they started flowing. I felt cared for and found so much comfort in that. She listened, listened, and then listened some more.

She let me say the ornery things I wanted to say, like how much I hated pregnant people and how mean God was to allow the pregnancy to happen just to let it end this way. She didn't judge or use trite sayings to ease my pain.

I was thankful Karen didn't make me pray or force Scripture on me. She suggested often that I journal my feelings, but she never got mad or disappointed when I didn't. She prayed for me, encouraged me, and validated my feelings. Our time together was a balm to my soul—and truly what got me through each day. For a year, Karen and I committed to our meetings. The first five months we met on my couch, since I couldn't bear to face the outside world, and then we slowly progressed to the back porch and finally to walking around my neighborhood or on a trail while we talked. She was so patient.

Karen was just what I needed: a friend to lean on and listen to me. A ray of hope. I can see now that God didn't leave me during that time. He waited patiently as the person he sent to me helped me find my way back to him.

She often says our relationship was set up for my healing but brought her healing as well. Karen was an unexpected answer to prayer, becoming my friend by way of an unfortunate sorority.

But just as unexpectedly, she taught me how to be a better friend. She served as an example to me in asking good questions, listening intently, sharing appropriately, and being truly present in my relationships.

She made me want to be more Christlike, and she showed me how.

A dark period brought us together. But now when we are together there is true Light.

Reflections

What qualities do I value most in a friend? Am I open to the women God may be sending to me in nontraditional ways?

One Beat at a Time

Lisa Howell

A friend loves at all times,
and a brother is born for a time of adversity.

Proverbs 17:17

I saw her for months and months before we met.

Though I was desperate for friends and was praying for them, I was also immersed in young motherhood. I was inwardly focused, busy, and insecure. I wasn't sure how to go about connecting with other women on a deeper level, especially when there were so many mommy things I was unsure of.

When Kyndall and I finally did meet while both volunteering for an event, I couldn't help but feel I'd wasted time I could've spent getting to know her. The energy was great between us, the friendship natural and fun. She made me want to be a better mother and a better friend. She handed down clothes to my child. *Why did it take me so long?*

I was sharing it all with my husband one date night, relishing the time to touch base and reconnect, when my phone quietly chirped. I'd found my groove as a mom, I told him, and was meeting uplifting, solid women. Life felt as even as it could get when strep throat, mountain lion sightings, and snowstorms were the winter norm in our mountain town. Cheers!

My cell phone chirped again.

My new friend was going to the hospital. At age thirty-seven, she was having a heart attack. I knew she hadn't felt well that week, and I knew dinner was over. Real friendship means using your own empty car seats on date night to take on someone else's kids for the foreseeable future.

A night of panic was followed by months of appointments, tests, and unanswered questions. It was a test of faith and of mental toughness. For us both. *After such a long drought, this was the friend I prayed for?* The words "Not fair!" passed before tear-weary eyes.

Being Kyndall's friend was going to mean facing her mortality every day. And my own. We turn off sad or uncomfortable news on television. But she was plunged into this with no remote to mute the uncertainty.

I learned about living one day at a time. I watched as Kyndall calmly prepared early for her own possible death. Wills. Plans. She asked me to continue scrapbooking her youngest daughter's life if something should happen to her. I had to decide to embrace the "if." To embrace *her*, fully.

I prayed for God to keep her safe. I have been a witness to the magnificence of her reliance on God and trust in his plan on an hourly basis. There was parenting on her agenda, not self-pity. My friend was disappointed to be told not to climb any more of our beloved Colorado peaks, that her heart couldn't take it. Yet to me she seemed to reach higher and higher every day.

I can't live her life for her, only with her—and with the God who chose to bring us together.

Thanks to Kyndall I know a different side of friendship and a different level of God's presence in the daily. Friendship is park play dates and crisply dressed mornings at MOPS and meal-making in a crisis. *God is with us.* Friendship is facing head-on the bloodshot eyes and phone calls that make you cringe, long after others have moved on. *God is with us.*

There is a certainty in our silent moments now. She is a gift to me. Today. And for every tomorrow she has. *God is with us.*

Reflections

Why have I befriended the friends I have? Do I ask more of my friends than I am willing to give of myself?

Shells

Ashley Larkin

I have loved you with an everlasting love;
I have drawn you with unfailing kindness.

Jeremiah 31:3

Kelly and I loaded the cars with our six children, beach towels, changes of clothes and shoes, pails and shovels, and lunch for the eight of us. There were books to read on the way, sunhats, raincoats, cameras, sunscreen, and child-sized sunglasses.

This was going to be an adventure.

Girls disbursed between full backseats, we were driving three hours for just one afternoon of play at the beach.

Kelly had recently moved to the Northwest, and though she and I had not been friends long, I already counted her among my favorite people. Bleary-eyed with a newborn and facing the start of school in just a few weeks, I didn't think I had room for another friend. And then I met Kelly.

My husband introduced us, having talked to her one night at a soccer practice. I was immediately drawn to Kelly's honesty, sincerity, and humor.

I was also compelled by the way she lived life with her children. She didn't flinch at driving to another state alone with them, learning the guitar, or packing up for last-minute picnics to the park. After years of play dates in basements and backyards, I found my heart crying, "Yes!" to the possibility of new adventures with my three girls and our new friends.

Kelly and I planned the trip to the beach after drawing sketches of vegetable gardens we would plant together. A trip to the coast would be simple and sweet, and I delighted in the promise of this day.

But as our time drew closer, I worried. Clara was not a good sleeper, and I imagined my overtired girl in a floppy hat, screaming at the loud crashing waves, the rain, the feel of sand.

More than Clara, I worried about me. I imagined myself overwhelmed by sandy mess, older children running into waves, younger ones playing on rocks and getting cut up by barnacles that cause funky bacterial infections. Would I crack and prove to Kelly that I was a very uncool mom after all?

I took a bite of sand-filled peanut butter sandwich and looked across the pile of blankets and towels to the friend I hardly knew and felt the risk of this adventure. *What if I offend her in how I handle a tantrum? What if I can't think of anything to say? What if, after spending a day together, Kelly doesn't like me as much as she'd thought?*

As I watched the kids collecting shells, I felt the roar of the ocean, squished the sand, and asked myself: Will you step out in faith in this new friendship, remembering you belong to an all-loving God who accepts you even if you're rejected? Or will you choose security that is not secure at all—built on the behavior of children, your "rightness" as a mom, or the opinions of a friend?

I looked up from my feet to four little girls with sticks in hand, writing their names together, free smiles stretching across round cheeks. I felt humbled by their pure hearts and lack of self-doubt.

I chose this risk. Home secures and accepts me, and a day in our backyard would have been easier. Yet here, on this summer day, I opened the gift picked for me by God.

He's given me the adventure of growing friendship and the blessing of Kelly, and more: his own solid presence that doesn't shift like the sand through my toes. Regardless of what happens in this or any other relationship, God accepts and loves me. He writes my name in big block letters that say *you are mine*.

Reflections

Do memories of childhood friendships inhibit or inspire how I go about connecting with other women now? Do I truly believe that God accepts me "warts and all" and that other women might too?

I'll Have What She's Having

Shannon Milholland

> Rejoice always . . . give thanks in all circum-
> stances; for this is God's will for you in Christ
> Jesus.
>
> 1 Thessalonians 5:16, 18

Ever since the first of my four beauties slid into my arms, my heart has been inspired to compose quirky songs. I sing about what we do and where we go. I sing as we clean, travel, or snuggle. I sing because of the joy that wells up in my heart.

When my youngest daughter Carynne was just old enough to walk, we were toddling one day to the backdrop of a cloudless Texas sky as I sang "Rynnie Roo" to the top of her blonde curls. Unbeknownst to me, another preschooler named Corinne was walking nearby with her mommy. Carynne and Corinne share the same nickname. The other Corinne looked up at her mom with pleading eyes and implored, "Would you sing me the Rynnie Roo song?"

That may have been what Corinne said, but what she meant was, "I'll have what she's having." She saw a mommy singing silly songs to her daughter. She wanted that for herself. Some day my Carynne will cringe at my singing, notice a more refined mother, and mutter to herself, "I'll have what she's having."

I too look at other gals, see the exterior of their lives, and desire what I see. From the outside my friend's husband,

118

children, home, or job seems superior to my own. I see only the positives, like eyeing a bank account just after payday without subtracting the bills from it. The sum looks large until you notice all the expenses it must cover.

My girlfriends possess amazing qualities. They have been blessed by God. However, when I look at them through the lens of jealousy I see only the deposits into their lives, none of the withdrawals from it.

I need girlfriends. We all do. Mothering is a lonely road to walk without the encouragement and support of other women. When I walk linked arm in arm with others, my journey as a mom is smoothed by their presence, prayers, and participation in my life.

I want to be a woman who attracts friends. So how can I? I have found I am most appealing when content with what I have and truly thankful for what God gives my friends. When I am this kind of woman, others flock. When I am not, they retreat.

Taking my eyes off Jesus is the primary cause of discontent, with envy the accelerant. I fail to praise if I'm too busy looking at someone else's blessings, circumstances, or finances to notice the symphony of blessings God is showering on me.

Jesus, today I will read off my own menu and not allow my eyes to wander to the next table. When my eyes are busy noticing all the ways you are working in my life, I count my blessings. I will walk flanked by friends. I will celebrate my friend's successes with her. I will rejoice as you bless her.

My heart will solidly declare, *I want what I'm having.*

Reflections

How has jealousy stood as a barrier, consciously or unconsciously, to loving my friends or making new ones? How can I make gratitude a constant state rather than an isolated event?

7

Time Out

God Is with Us . . .
When We Feel Overwhelmed

For God has not given us a spirit of fear, but of
power and of love and of a sound mind.

2 Timothy 1:7 NKJV

One baby in a parking lot overwhelmed me. I was such
a rookie I couldn't figure out how to open his stroller.
Then there were two, crying at night at the drive-through
pharmacy, one hungry, one weak from pneumonia, and me
so ravenous I considered the dead Cheerios at the bottom of
my purse. I was sure *that* was the pinnacle of pressure.

But then there was a third, arriving early and under two
and a half pounds. I prayed on the way to the hospital twice
a day that he'd be alive, pumped eight times a day for milk he
relied on, parented two other sons under five, and continued
to help lead my MOPS group.

I might have truly imploded had I not seen her that day: my friend crouched in the church hallway, eyes wet, having just dropped her child off after a raging battle. *Another* raging battle.

"I don't know how to do this," she said flatly, "and today I just don't want to."

I could only embrace her. Tell her she was exactly the mom God wanted for her children. And then walk into the bathroom and bawl. For her. For me. For the boiling over that I knew was a part of so many mothers' lives.

Like poking holes in a potato before baking it, releasing a little steam that day kept me from breaking apart. Thanks to God's hand on my hunched shoulder, I could keep my eyes on what was necessary and what was possible that day.

Necessary and possible.

We can't do it all, every day. But we *can* ask God each day to grow our peace and perseverance for the times we feel paralyzed by our circumstances.

Galatians 5:22–23 tells us "the fruit of the Spirit is love, joy, peace, forbearance, kindness, goodness, faithfulness, gentleness and self-control." When we hold tightly to Christ, he will grow those qualities in us, qualities that we need when we are overwhelmed.

Mary was an unwed mother. Hannah faced infertility. Mary and Martha anguished over a dying brother. Ruth left all she knew to care for her mother-in-law. Rahab and Queen Esther both faced life-and-death choices. Mary Magdalene searched for the Savior. The widow of Zarephath (with her son) was destitute.

Surely each woman felt besieged at various moments. But they all managed a resilient peace amid the turmoil when they kept their eyes on "the God of all comfort" (2 Cor. 1:3). Paul managed to call him that during his exciting and painful life as a missionary.

Fear and fatigue can obscure the comfort that God offers his overwhelmed daughters and even obscure his presence altogether.

We fear we aren't enough, that we're not doing this mom thing right—certainly we aren't doing it like *her*—and how in the world can we do the next sixteen years if we can't do *today*? We're biting off more than any mom can chew if we're worried about the future and comparing ourselves to others. We must "say with confidence, 'The Lord is my helper; I will not be afraid'" (Heb. 13:6).

Like fear, fatigue is real and insidious. It can make us snap at the little things and put us in danger of some big things, such as being too tired to dispense medicine correctly. God wants us to rest, like he did on the seventh day of creating the universe. Jesus tells us, "Come to me, all you who are weary and burdened, and I will give you rest" (Matt. 11:28).

Rest is improbable some days. Pray for God's strength. Don't arrange your day in such a way that defeat is imminent. You can handle one more day without going to the store.

If feeling overwhelmed is a way of life, talk to your doctor. Anxiety and postpartum depression are common in young mothers and can be helped. There's no shame in seeking answers for your childrearing questions or for your own mental and physical health.

When it all just seems too much, God is there. "Neither height nor depth, nor anything else in all creation, will be able to separate us from the love of God" (Rom. 8:39). Not even our own anxious hearts or layered responsibilities.

> *God, I'm snowed under. Help me take life one*
> *shovelful at a time, and show my children*
> *that I rely on your strength, not my own.*

A Necessary Shift

Tracey Bianchi

He said to me, "My grace is sufficient for you, for
my power is made perfect in weakness." Therefore
I will boast all the more gladly about my weaknesses, so that Christ's power may rest on me.

2 Corinthians 12:9

I once thought parenthood would be all snuggles and naps.
All those moms who stress over fevers and feeding
schedules must really be drama queens. Babies are born via
a flawless adoption or the help of an earthy midwife, and
nursing is a breeze, because, after all, women have been doing
this for centuries.

And why *wouldn't* your perfectly capable husband roll up
in a hybrid car with a nontoxic, über-safe car seat and drive
you away from the hospital into eternal parenting bliss?

Insert scratchy record sound here.

My entry into the world of motherhood was utterly jarring.
I tried to orchestrate the whole affair down to the twinkle stars
bedding, only to find this new chapter would be anything but
matching-gingham bliss. My birth experience went opposite
of my plans. The only thing that went right was that a baby
was indeed born.

My husband and I headed home a few days later, grip-
ping the wheel in a pounding thunderstorm while fearing
the next wind gust would swoosh our little family across
the highway. Feeding our son was a nightmare, and he was

colicky, a foreign word I quickly discovered meant I would never go more than an hour without a screaming infant for the next six weeks—unless he was so tired from howling that he zonked out.

Exhaustion and depression picked up where the pain from my stitches left off.

I remember sitting on my back stoop holding my son and sobbing. He was also having a moment, and I watched as a tear slipped from my chin, hit his forehead, slid down his nose, and blended with his tears.

And at that very moment I officially lost it.

I clutched my son and just sobbed for half an hour until, finally lifting my head, I simply said, "I surrender."

"I give up. God, it's your turn to be in control," I said, confessing that I really had no idea how to parent a two-month-old, let alone the surly adolescent I was told would later come.

I had reached the end of me.

So I drew in a breath and gave the whole sloppy mess over to God. Nothing immediately changed. I still stood ankle deep in tears, exhaustion, and the fringes of depression. But a dramatic, necessary shift we all must make had finally occurred. I released my perfectly laid plans and my insecurities to God. His heart for my son, and for me, would pull us through.

Motherhood renders many of us about as weak and needy as they come. Our preconceived notions of parenting—it starts the moment we get the Pottery Barn Kids catalog, those ideas that motherhood is tidy and perfect—barely get us out of the hospital. We struggle with everything from depression to depletion to learning how to manage the life of a person who cannot even talk yet. Even in the commercials that try to make motherhood look messy, the mom is too pretty and the house is airy and pristine.

125

So we struggle. We try to make sense of our own less-than-perfect parenting lives, and we're afraid of looking needy by asking for help. I had to let go. I had to see and trust that God's abundant grace could bring us through the entire journey (even the mayhem of parenting a middle schooler).

As I rose from my back porch that afternoon, my son still cried, nap schedules were still erratic, sippy cups still broke—and three babies later my life is an even bigger mess of dirty kids.

And I still cry.

But I am okay with telling people the truth about how I'm doing. Okay with not knowing how tomorrow will go. I "go to the stoop" constantly in my heart, turning life over to God.

I let him stand in as the expert, and I cling less to my own expectations. I've settled into the passenger seat while the grace-filled God of this world drives the minivan.

Reflections

What false expectations did I bring to parenting? Do I see surrendering to God as making me weaker or stronger?

Yes, You Can

Julia Attaway

Ask and it will be given to you; seek and you will
find; knock and the door will be opened to you.

Matthew 7:7

"Elizabeth," I said with forced calm to my purple-faced
banshee, "Mommy needs a time-out."

With my last shred of self-control I scooped up the baby
and stalked into my bedroom and shut the door.

A little harder than necessary.

Elizabeth stood in the hallway and continued her tantrum.
She was a precocious hysteric, capable of two-hour screaming fits. I'd already survived a couple rounds that morning
and wasn't up for more. *Lord, give me patience or make her
stop!* I prayed crankily, before remembering to thank him for
the invention of doors.

I gave baby John some attention, and he smiled apprecia-
tively. My daughter's storm raged on. After a while I mustered
the energy to reenter the tempest—only to discover that the
1930s-era Art Deco doorknob to my room had jammed. And
so there I was on one side of the door, with my tempestuous
toddler on the other.

"Elizabeth," I called through the keyhole, somewhat
abashed, "Mommy's stuck. I want to hold you, but the door
won't open. Can you open it from your side?" Intrigued that

127

Mommy needed her help, my daughter hiccupped her way to a lower decibel and tried turning the knob.

Nothing doing.

I assessed the situation. I might be able to remove the hinges, but that probably wouldn't allow me to remove the door. Chattering through the keyhole with false cheer, I used the file from a nail clippers to unscrew the plate around the doorknob. I took off the knob, then stared stupidly at the mechanism. Should I push out the shaft connecting to the knob on the other side? What if I needed it and Elizabeth couldn't put it back?

Puzzled, I sat down and nursed John, who was getting hungry. *Okay Lord, I can't do this alone. I need your help.* I prayed and waited for a convenient miracle, but nothing happened.

I thought of calling the super for our building, but the phone was in the living room. I wondered if Elizabeth could hold it up to the keyhole so I could push the numbers with a pencil. Probably not.

I prayed again. No answer.

I knocked on the floor for ten minutes to get the attention of our downstairs neighbors. Apparently they weren't home.

By now I'd been locked in the bedroom for an hour and had run out of ideas. It was mid-afternoon, and Andrew wasn't due home from work until seven. *Lord, what if Elizabeth wanders off and gets hurt? I really need your help!* Still no answer.

John cooed, and I looked down at his smile. I realized with a start that Elizabeth's tantrum had stopped long ago. My *I-can't-take-this*-ness was a thing of the past, replaced by the puzzle of the door.

God had given me a way out of my trauma all right, by letting me get stuck in another way.

Laughing—at myself, for wanting God to whisk away my troubles, and at God for his bemusing certainty that I can handle more than I want to—I went to the door and called to Elizabeth to stand back. With a surge of courage I pushed the shaft of the doorknob out, and heard it clatter on the floor. I jammed the nail clippers into the gaping hole and turned. And lo and behold, the door I thought was impossibly locked opened.

My *I-can't-take-this* attitude was really just code for *I don't want motherhood to be this hard*. Thankfully God gives me the courage to hear his quiet voice telling me, "Yes, you can."

Reflections

Am I able to see the lighter side of being overwhelmed, while I'm overwhelmed? What are my reactions really saying—and saying to my kids—in these moments?

Seeking Peace

Rachel Swenson Balducci

May the God of hope fill you with all joy and
peace as you trust in him, so that you may overflow with hope by the power of the Holy Spirit.

Romans 15:13

O n my very first Mother's Day, my six-month-old son
and his daddy got me a camcorder. The three of us:
Paul, sweet baby Ethan, and I, spent the day enjoying life as
a little family. That was an awesome day. It felt a bit strange
and surreal to be celebrating Mother's Day as a mother, to
have people honoring me for being in that category.

Last Mother's Day wasn't quite as awesome. Paul and I
spent the day at the emergency room with our not-quite-two-
year-old Henry. Henry had broken his femur at the family
Mother's Day picnic. The three of us: me, Paul, and our sweet
baby Henry, spent the night at the hospital. The next day
Henry got a cast that stayed on for more than seven weeks.

This Mother's Day was somewhere in between. It was not
a bad day, not even close. Now that my standards of a "bad
Mother's Day" include the baby being encased in a full-body
cast, it is going to take a lot for me to ever deem another
Mother's Day as truly bad. *Please, Lord, protect us all!*

But it was not the happy-go-lucky day of years past either.
We are in a challenging season right now, a season of taking
things one day at a time, and really, some days I do better
assessing my life on an hourly basis.

I know this season won't last forever. At this point, I have to remind myself that we have a tiny newborn, which means I should be doing very little soul-searching in general. Rarely does any good come from a sleep-deprived mother analyzing the way things are.

Some days are just going to be harder than others.

And yet, somehow things are quite wonderful at the same time.

In the midst of sleepless nights and protecting a tiny baby from the loving arms of her toddler brother while helping an older boy with homework and getting someone else ready for a field trip, I am grateful for it all. I look forward to the day, even a few months from now, when we are back in a better groove, but I take today with gratitude too.

In my journey as a mother, and as a Christian, I am learning that all these externals will change. Some days are nearly perfect; other days are not.

The days may change, but my interior state should not. For better and for worse, life seasons will come and go. In the midst of the ease *and* the strain, I can still have peace.

Today the pace is frantic; at some point, it won't be. Either way, I seek peace. While life might not always be as ordered as I prefer, I can always have peace in my soul. I just have to remember to seek it. As mothers, one of the most important things we can do is to bring that peace into our homes, a peace not compromised by the details of our days.

"The peace of the world meant that I had all that I desired, the peace of Christ that I desired no more than all I had," writes Fr. Bede Jarrett. "The peace of Christ depended wholly, under the grace of God, on the attitude of the soul."[1]

When I have moments of feeling tired or agitated, or even times when I am fine physically but emotionally spread thin, I

1. Bede Jarrett, *Meditations for Layfolk* (reprint, Whitefish, MT: Kessinger, 2003), 298.

redirect my soul to its maker. It sounds lofty, but it's actually very simple. I have to remind myself, in moments of sadness or insecurity or just plain frustration, that as the psalmist proclaims, only in God is my soul at rest, and only in him comes my salvation.

Remembering the heart of the matter, that God made me and loves me, always helps me take a deep breath and get a grip. It gives me perspective—and that, when we are seeking peace, is half the battle.

Reflections

What's my biggest challenge to finding God's sustaining peace—before a situation rages? Do I try?

Sometimes I Just Wanna Quit

Renee Swope

> You have given me your shield of victory.
> Your right hand supports me;
> your help has made me great.
>
> Psalm 18:35 NLT

I love my kids, but I haven't always *liked* being a mom.
Once my boys became toddlers who wouldn't listen
to me or do what I told them, I kind of panicked. I looked
around at other moms who seemed to know what they were
doing and wondered, *What is wrong with me?*

Their children seemed to listen when they told them no.
Why wouldn't my child keep *his* hands to himself or stay
in the cart at the grocery store? Why did he not understand
when I told him I could not buy everything his little hand
could touch? How come no one told me that being a mom
would be so hard?

I felt like such a failure.

Almost every day, I would compare how I felt on the inside
to other moms who looked like they had it all together on
the outside.

I held up my feelings of inadequacy and thoughts of insecurity in contrast to moms who dressed their children in
matching outfits and adorned themselves with attitudes of
grace and wisdom. I wondered how in the world they pulled

it off with a smile. I could barely get a shower, get my kids dressed, and get us out the door before lunch.

I just wanted to quit.

One day I came home from running too many errands with two very tired and fussy kids.

I put them down for an early nap and started looking for pink construction paper so I could write "I QUIT" on it. I'd decided to turn in my "pink slip" to my husband when he came home from work that day. It was just too hard, and I was tired of feeling like I would never be "good enough" as a mom.

But what I needed was a new place to start. I didn't really start becoming the mom God created me to be until the day I was ready to quit. That afternoon I fell on my knees before God and choked out the words, "I can't do this."

And in that place of surrender, his peace came over me. His gentleness calmed my nerves. I felt like God bent down over me and spoke to my heart: *You are right, Renee. In your strength and through your perspective, you can't do this. But with my promises, my presence, and my power, all things are possible. I will help you become a great mom.*

I needed God in my mothering. But my habit of comparing myself to other moms was like a third voice drowning out his and critically mimicking my own. I had to—and still have to—surrender those comparisons to make them powerless and focus instead on the strength he gives me.

Looking back on that day, I'm reminded of Psalm 19:35: "You have given me your shield of victory. Your right hand supports me; your help has made me great" (NLT).

When we acknowledge that on our own we are a mess, God rushes to our side to help us. He bends down to show us that with his grace, wisdom, and guidance, we can become the mom he is calling us to be, the mom our kids need us to be, and the mom we want to be.

That often doesn't have much to do with the mom we just saw at the store.

Reflections

Does the outward appearance and actions of other moms and their kids overwhelm me and breed doubt? How can I quiet my own voice of disapproval?

Running Away, to Him

Keri Wyatt Kent

Then, because so many people were coming and
going that they did not even have a chance to eat,
he said to them, "Come with me by yourselves to a
quiet place and get some rest."

Mark 6:31

I grab hot, clean plates from the dishwasher, setting them
on the counter before they scald my fingers. My one-
year-old in the high chair delicately pinches one Cheerio at
a time. Half make it to his mouth, the rest fall to the floor
or his lap. I sigh, cutting up a banana for both of us. I stand,
nibbling, watching him.

When's the last time I sat down to eat?

I'm weary, feeling inadequate. I'm sucked into conflicts
between my kids. How do you explain to a toddler not to
knock over his sister's blocks? Work and parenting obliga-
tions yank me in two directions. My husband's long hours
leave me lonely and overwhelmed.

I've lived a full day before breakfast, awakened at 5:30 by
my daughter, crying and tangled in wet sheets for the first
time since she'd given up nighttime diapers a week ago. I'd
pulled off her wet pj's, wrapped her in a big towel, and offered
patient, reassuring words. "Is it okay that I had an accident?"
she had wailed with her typical drama.

I've got the kids dressed, sheets changed and laundered,
and dishwasher emptied—almost.

My husband showers, and I'm listening for the water to shut off. He's promised to spend the day with the kids. I'm craving solitude so badly I ache, but in my heart guilt wrestles with that desire for rest.

Selfish as it felt, I'd asked for a day off from the squabbles and time-outs, from inexplicable tantrums (mine and the kids'), from diapers and potty training and wet pajamas. I need to be with Jesus in a quiet place. He is here, in the duties and noise. But the desire within me to go away for a while—that's him too, calling for me.

Of course, my daughter is being incredibly sweet—making me doubt my escape plan. She sits on the couch, "reading" a favorite Curious George book to her toy Barney. Barney sits on her lap, gazing blankly, as Melanie animatedly tells the story.

I pour cereal into a plastic bowl. She shuffles in, setting Barney on the stool at the kitchen island, and eats her cereal. As I put the milk back in the fridge, she notices the leftover pudding within.

"Can I have pudding?"

Something in me just deflates. I am so weary. Besides, pudding is mostly milk, right?

"Okay," I say, pulling out a dish, plunking it beside her empty cereal bowl. Melanie looks at me in shock.

"Why did you say yes?" she asks, not waiting for an answer as she digs into the soft, cold chocolate.

"Because I'm tired of fighting," I sigh. "Don't you get tired of fighting?"

"No," she says calmly, licking the spoon.

"Did you want me to say, 'no pudding'?" It's come to this: I'm asking my preschooler for parenting advice.

"Yes," she says, finishing it off.

I just shake my head, wipe her face with a paper towel as she squirms down, grabs Barney, and runs off to play. I wipe down my son's face and hands and take him out of the high chair.

Later, despite a tearful good-bye, I leave and run to Jesus, taking him up on his invitation to rest. No one says "Mommy!" to me the whole time. I walk, pray, read my Bible, and write in my journal, uninterrupted. So many women don't ask to go, even when Jesus asks. They suffer or pout or complain, but never really ask for what they need. But I choose to obey Jesus, knowing time with him will make me a better mom.

Stepping away, I can laugh at the thought of my daughter licking that pudding spoon, asking for boundaries. I ask too, and am replenished, reminded that I'm not just a mom, but also a daughter—of a God who loves me.

Reflections

Do I feel guilty taking time off from my mothering? Why? How else can I refuel when I feel drained?

Confessions
of an Unhappy Mother

Hayley DiMarco

Both good and bad come from the mouth of the
Most High God.

Lamentations 3:38 GW

When we first brought our Addy home from the hospital
I was a wreck.

I can remember sitting up at three in the morning, trying
to get her to latch on, my husband watching and wishing he
could do something, but being helpless.

I was so tired, so not in love with this little stranger. I looked
at Michael through tear-filled eyes and asked in all sincerity,
"Do you think they would take her back? If we went to the
hospital would they take her back?"

And for a brief second I was filled with the anticipation of
a "Yes, let's do it. It was all just a big mistake, honey." But that
fantasy was soon dashed by the resigned shake of his head.

My comfortable life, my sleeping in, my making my own
schedule, my daily naps—they were all gone and replaced
with servitude.

I'll be honest: every day of motherhood reveals more and
more of my selfishness and self-centeredness. Yet God continues to love me—and that to me is the biggest blessing of
being a mom.

For most of my life I've seen the difficult things happening to me and around me as, well, bad! Bad for me, bad news, bad pain. I have a pretty good idea of what makes me happy, and it isn't serving others and trying hard and being patient.

But then something revolutionary hit my life: I started to give God more power. Well, not actually give him power, but to accept the power he already has. I started to see him as God with a big G, and not just little god that's occasionally involved in my life.

I started to accept the fact that nothing happens except as he allows it for my good. What a concept! The idea that both good and bad come from God, not to destroy me, but to change me, to teach me, and to grow me was the key to *all* that happened in my life, even things I'd deemed as suffering.

It came when I was reading a book on the attributes of God, *The Knowledge of the Holy* by A. W. Tozer. In his book I read this Scripture: "Who was it who spoke and it came into being? It was the Lord who gave the order. Both good and bad come from the mouth of the Most High God" (Lam. 3:37–38 GW).

And suddenly I got it.

If everything comes from God, and not from the enemy, then all suffering is a beautiful thing, because everything from God is perfect (see Ps. 18:30). Wow! What wonderful freedom, hope in suffering, and certainty that it is all meant for good—and will only serve to mature me, teach me, and help me.

With this outlook, life took a dramatic turn for me. My sorrow became joy as I saw the cleansing power of trials and the powerful hand of God in every late-night interruption and every plaintive cry.

When I saw God as actively involved in my daily life, there was nothing that wasn't beautiful, nothing that wasn't perfect for me, and nothing that could make me unhappy ever again.

It's a precious lesson I remind myself, and my beautiful daughter, daily.

Reflections

Do I see God in the good and the bad? How would doing this more consistently challenge the role I give God in my daily life?

8

On the Move

God Is with Us . . . in Our Work

She sets about her work vigorously;
her arms are strong for her tasks.

Proverbs 31:17

*C*ouldn't be. Not yet.

I tried to ignore the faint rustling, but momma radar was already well honed. The baby was awake upstairs.

He hadn't gotten the day's schedule, didn't realize an hour of sleep and a long to-do list remained.

Clinching my eyes tight, I tried willing him back to la-la land. *When am I going to get my work done?* I trudged up to get my little man, frustrated. His smile through the crib slats melted my heart yet again. I could easily see God in those blue eyes. So why did I feel so alone when it came to completing anything?

If I was honest with myself, I wasn't looking to find God in my deadlines or my dishwater. Having a son was clearly a miracle. Having a career or taking care of my home—that was just what people did. So God in mothering was clear to me. God in my time card or in making dinner, not so much.

At first.

God is in our daily work, whether that work takes us downtown or down on the floor. He can illuminate what our work *is* when we turn to him for help in making decisions. Our time is time he's given us. Once I started seeing it that way, and asking how he wanted me to spend it, I didn't tend to worry as much about checking the "done" box.

Make no mistake, nothing gets me going like accomplishing something—and work deadlines are real things—but God's got to be in the accomplishing or it's like eating a donut for energy: only fleeting satisfaction. "So whether you eat or drink or whatever you do, do it all for the glory of God" (1 Cor. 10:31).

God doesn't leave us alone in our tasks. He knows having children causes an identity shift, if not a crisis, in most women. We are told, "Do not lose heart. . . . For our light and momentary troubles are achieving for us an eternal glory that far outweighs them all" (2 Cor. 4:16–17). We may miss having a title and a paycheck, or we may see the title and the paycheck differently now that we must leave little ones behind each day. Even on the best of days, work is draining. We anticipate, we hope, we question our purposes and our methods, and we continually seek to juggle and balance. The unseen work constantly churns within us. But God sees it.

Strong women abound in the Bible, each with her own work to do. Hannah was needed to be the mother of Samuel, and his long-awaited conception led him to great purpose in God's kingdom (see 1 Sam. 1–3). Deborah was needed to be a judge in Israel; her ability to direct and delegate with wisdom led the Israelites to victory (see Judg. 4–5).

In listening to God's voice in their work—whether they were seeking him, pleading with him, or praising him—both women were able to lead others to him in the course of their responsibilities.

Whether in the office or on the playground, "in the same way, let your light shine before others, that they may see your good deeds and glorify your Father in heaven" (Matt. 5:16). Our work-born busyness can serve to isolate us from others, but Scripture tells us every person in our path is a chance to show love:

> Speaking the truth in love, we will grow to become in every respect the mature body of him who is the head, that is, Christ. From him the whole body, joined and held together by every supporting ligament, grows and builds itself up in love, as each part does its work. (Eph. 4:15–16)

Proverbs 31 is a well-known praise for all a woman does. Its litany of tasks might seem exhausting, but I think it's exhilarating to see that God knows all the often-hidden work we do, in and out of the home. The cornerstone of all these activities is revering God.

We seek the "right" way to do it all. But parenting is an inexact science. Co-workers will not always agree with our decisions. So we do our best and seek God's approval, not that of society or even that of friends or in-laws. He has work for each of us to do. Success and honor and worth come not from the task, but from letting him be God over them all.

> *Lord, I want you to reign over my busy life.*
> *Show me your will for me in this job, with this*
>   *child, on this day.*

A Cubicle (or a Room)
of One's Own

Karen Halvorsen Schreck

I can do everything through Christ, who gives me
strength.

Philippians 4:13 NLT

I'm sitting in my quiet cubicle writing copy about expensive
chocolate ("enrobed" is the word *du jour*, as in: "mouth-
watering caramel *enrobed* in decadent layers of dark chocolate bliss"), when I get the phone call.

"You have a referral," the adoption caseworker says in
her familiar southern accent. "A girl. Born twelve days ago
in Guatemala City."

I press the phone so hard to my ear that I hear the beat of
my heart there, reverberating off plastic.

I have a daughter.

Or to put it another way: I might actually be a mother.

I am also, of course, a writer. I kick into high writer-gear,
scribbling down all the caseworker can share about this baby
for whom my husband and I have waited for over a year. For
our whole adult lives, it seems. My handwriting—purple ink
scrawled haphazardly across a yellow legal pad—is shaky:
6 lbs., 5 ounces. Already in foster care.

I spend the rest of my workday carrying the news of my
daughter's birth like a secret life inside me. Fragile as a butter-
fly's wing, her existence feels, and as miraculously beautiful.

Weeks before, during Advent, I read Mary's Song of Praise. Now the Magnificat returns to me:

"My soul glorifies the Lord and my spirit rejoices in God my Savior, for he has been mindful of the humble state of his servant. From now on all generations will call me blessed, for the Mighty One has done great things for me—holy is his name" (Luke 1:46–49).

At home that night, I tell my husband our news in person. We burst into tears—our first-ever tears of joy.

Then months pass.

The wait to bring our daughter home is excruciatingly long, exquisitely meaningful.

Finally one day in May, we return with her, transforming a would-be baby shower into her welcome home party.

For weeks, I remain in Magnificat-mode, astonished by the miracle of this baby and crying tears of joy. I think things like: *Just look at her eyes moving beneath her closed lids—what could she possibly be dreaming? Listen to how she laughs, how she cries. Feel her silken skin. Smell . . . how she smells—yes, even that! Be. With. Her. Now!*

Then one day, I find myself crying again.

Not tears of joy.

And it comes upon me—that "down the rabbit hole" feeling. Alice-like, I am lost in this wonderland that is suddenly not so perfectly wonderful. My husband, a college prof, has gone back to work. We are often alone, my daughter and me.

She proves more than a fantasy; she proves a person. Her immune system is off. She falls victim to one virus after the next. Sleep is not always there for the taking. Most of my friends are single or are childfree (versus childless). And I'm a writer . . . aren't I?

One bleak fall day my daughter, sedated with Simulac, takes her afternoon nap. I tiptoe from her room, carefully shutting the door. It creaks like always. But today she doesn't wake back up.

Instead of going downstairs to sterilize the drippy, souring bottle in my hand, I enter the empty bedroom—the one we hope will be another child's one day. I sit down in this little space that, for now, is my own. My tidy, quiet cubicle, I think, though I have left that particular office behind.

But I have not left myself.

I take out a journal. I make a vow: whenever my daughter naps, no matter what (well, *mostly* no matter what), I will take time for this other self that is also me. I will write.

I am not Alice after all.

I sense God standing there, looking with favor upon my complexity.

Reflections

How do I identify myself? By workplace? By offspring? By my mood today? What gifts or talents do I have that I want to continue nurturing?

Bringing God into It

Angie Weszely

LORD, you alone are my portion and my cup;
  you make my lot secure.
The boundary lines have fallen for me in pleasant
    places;
  surely I have a delightful inheritance.

                                        Psalm 16:5–6

I'm reading a novel on my iPhone as I walk home from the train, because I'm so exhausted from my day of work that I just need to escape. I want to hurry home to see my four-year-old son, but I'm also laughing out loud from this book and it feels great. I slow my pace a little, just to try to transition. I see my husband and son on the front porch, and Noah yells, "Mommy's home!"

Okay, this is even more energizing than my book.

It's the beginning of summer vacation and the first time he was with our new nanny. I sit him on my lap and ask, "How was your first day with Courtney?" He thinks for a few seconds then puts one thumb up and one thumb down.

I don't even ask why; my heart just plummets into this guilty-mom place that I still don't have figured out. I suddenly know I've made a terrible mistake, and my anxious thoughts begin. *What was I thinking, hiring a nanny for thirty-six hours a week? I should have supplemented day camp, because he's used to being with other kids at preschool. Now I'm worried he's going to have a miserable summer. Should I take more time off to spend with him?*

But then, as the story of the day unfolds, it starts to become clear that the thumbs-down part of his response is because Courtney had to give him a time-out, and he feels bad about it. The rational part of my brain believes that, but I still have to talk my emotions off the cliff.

I ask him several more questions throughout the evening. "What did you do? Do you like spending time with Courtney?" Only after he tells me three times in three different ways that he had a great day and is looking forward to tomorrow can I feel myself relaxing.

For the thousandth time since my son was born, I check in with God to see if I'm doing the right thing by having someone else watch my child while I am working. And for the thousandth time, he gently reminds me of the way he led me to this season of my life and that he has set the boundary lines for me in pleasant places.

I remember the years of infertility after my daughter was born and the way God directed my career path. He reminds me how I prayed that if he was going to allow me to get pregnant with a second child, it would be before I was asked to take the lead at work. Then he takes me back to viewing the positive pregnancy test, realizing that I had conceived during the first week of my new job, and my husband saying, "I guess God wants you to do both."

I wish this was a story from my past and I could share my victory over this area, but this happened yesterday. So I am still bringing God into it, tearing up as I write this. I love my kids, and I love what I do. I believe with all my heart that God has called me to both, so every day I lean on him to show me how to navigate the complexities and balance the priorities.

He is my portion, the one in whom I find security and strength.

Reflections

When I struggle with making decisions—or the ones already made—how can I more consistently bring God into my confusion?

Do We Have to Hurry, Mommy?

Jenne Acevedo

> So I commend the enjoyment of life, because there
> is nothing better for a person under the sun than
> to eat and drink and be glad. Then joy will ac-
> company them in their toil all the days of the life
> God has given them under the sun.
>
> Ecclesiastes 8:15

Mommy, do we have to hurry?" my four-year-old daughter asked as we walked out of the house on our way
to the store.

My first thought was, *Of course not, we are just going
to get groceries.* Then it hit me: I often tell her to hurry. She
wanted a heads-up.

I tell my daughter to hurry and clean her room. I tell my
boys to hurry and get in the car to go to school. I tell my
son to hurry up and finish his dinner since the rest of us are
already done. I tell my daughter to buckle her car seat quickly
so we can go. And I always seem to be in a hurry when I'm
driving. Perhaps I need to learn to slow down.

I challenged myself to keep patience at the forefront of
my mind one day as I took my daughter on several errands.
As usual, she took her time getting in and out of the car,
tiptoeing on the curb in each parking lot, walking into each
store and looking around at whatever sparkly or pink item
caught her eye.

Instead of pushing her along, I was patient. I even pointed out curbs she missed and let her try on some jewelry. We had a great time together running errands. We slowly explored the stores and even found some fun and inexpensive treasures. I hugged her supertight after dumping our bags at the front door and told her how proud I was of her behavior.

But I think the big reason she was able to behave so well was because *I* was behaving well. I chose to go about my work with a different attitude and had a great day with my precious little girl.

Jesus was busy with his ministry too, but he was never in a hurry. He asked his disciples to follow him, but he didn't say, "Hurry up and follow me." He asked people what they needed, but he didn't look at his watch while they explained their ailments. When he went away to pray, he didn't rush to get there so he could get on to the next important miracle.

Paul said, "Live a life filled with love, following the example of Christ" (Eph. 5:2 NLT). Jesus walked. Jesus stopped. Jesus listened. Contrast that with my day of running, impatiently stopping at red lights, and halfheartedly listening to my son tell me about his day at school while checking my email on my phone.

The root of my hurry: I must be useful and scheduled. I like to have a plan, execute it, and move on. If I can get the kids off to school early, I can have more time to do my Bible study and a load of laundry before rushing to my dental appointment. I *think* I must finish my daily to-do list, even though more tasks will be waiting for me tomorrow.

There are always things to do, and some must be done more quickly than others. But constant hurry sucks the joy out of life.

I desire to follow the challenge set forth by Paul: "Be very careful, then, how you live—not as unwise but as wise, making the most of every opportunity" (Eph. 5:15–16).

My little girl likes to spend time with me no matter where we are. When I take the extra time to enjoy being together too, she feels special and cherished.

That's worth more to me than any completed task or all the extra minutes in the world.

Reflections

What does my pace of life say about my priorities? At home and at work, how can I better live out the focus Jesus embodied?

From the Muck to the Rock

Stephanie Walter

> He lifted me out of the slimy pit,
>   out of the mud and mire;
> he set my feet on a rock
>   and gave me a firm place to stand.
>
> Psalm 40:2

I should have known I was in trouble when I burst into tears at the grocery store.

My list simply read "chips," and the multitude of colorful, puffy bags on the shelves overwhelmed me. Tortilla? Spicy? Rippled? Plain? Feeling foolish, I grabbed the bag closest to me, made my purchases, and raced to the safety of my car where I let the tears flow freely.

I'm just tired, I thought. I had recently returned to my full-time job as a high school teacher after becoming a mom to a baby girl who didn't like to sleep.

At all.

I had resigned myself to nursing her throughout the night. Her 4 a.m. feeding time became my wake-up call for another nineteen-hour day. I numbly used these early-morning hours to fold laundry, grade papers, and jolt myself awake by chugging diet soda.

I didn't realize it at first, but sleep deprivation exacerbated the onset of postpartum depression. I kept going. As I prayed for relief, I felt God nudging me, *This wasn't what we had planned, remember?*

I remembered. Vaguely.

Before this point in my life, I had never questioned my plan to quit whatever job I had to devote myself fully to mothering. But a funny thing happened on the way. I fell in love with energy-filled ninth graders and the creative outlet working in the classroom provided.

I was good at teaching.

Surely God didn't gift me in an area only to ask me to give it up. I had just completed a master's degree, for crying out loud.

Cry out loud is exactly what I did for two years, as I wrestled with God on the matter. During that time, I was one mud-splattered, drained, sad woman, unable to climb up out of the slimy pit I had become stuck in.

The push and pull between the dream God had planted in my heart and love for the career I had cultivated resulted in an identity crisis. I loved teaching, and I couldn't imagine walking away from "Mrs. Walter, English teacher." I had spent seven years championing the brilliance of *Romeo and Juliet* and *To Kill a Mockingbird* to funny, dramatic, precious students. I panicked at the thought of walking away.

Who was I if I wasn't a teacher?

Still, I kept hearing God whisper to my heart, *This is not my plan for you. For now, you aren't meant to give your heart to both pursuits at once.*

I tried several pitiful approaches to change God's mind. "Lord, would you fill me with your Spirit of joy?" But joy doesn't come easily to an overtired, unbalanced mom. Then I prayed for more energy. "God, please empower me to do the job you've given me." God reminded me that while his hand of blessing had been on my teaching, he wanted me to move to a different focus now.

Finally, I wimped out with the prayer of comparison. "But God, I see lots of other good teachers who are also great moms! Why can't I be both?"

I knew the response: *Because my plan for you is specific to you.*

Finally, I softened to God's prompting and went home to stay for a while. The depression lifted. I was able to see clearly what God had been telling me. I am his daughter, and that defines who I am. I'm in trouble if I tie my worth to my job, my kids, or my role as a wife for that matter.

My worth is tied to the Rock who never changes, and that beats the muck of exhaustion and overwork any day.

Reflections

Do I believe that God can and will show me what's best for me and my family? How has my decision to work outside the home, or to stay home with my children, challenged my physical and emotional health?

From Guilt to Grace

Laura Lee Groves

My grace is sufficient for you, for my power is
made perfect in weakness.

2 Corinthians 12:9

I sat at the computer with one ear trained on the little boys in the next room. Armed with their little trays and butter tubs full of Cheerios, they had settled down to watch *Reading Rainbow*.

I could stand and take three steps and see both of them. I could hear the slightest noise from the next room. They were busy and happy. Surely I could take thirty minutes to get some work done. I had a deadline, after all.

A few minutes passed with my eyes riveted to the screen, my fingers flying. Then I heard oh-so-close to my ear, "Mama."

No panic, no fear, just "Mama."

I blinked and turned left to see my two-and-a-half-year-old looking earnestly at me.

"Mama. Come."

"Is something wrong?" I asked.

"No."

He shook his head. Then he grabbed my hand from the keyboard.

"Mama. Come."

158

He pulled me up and led me into the next room. He sat down behind his little tray with his Cheerios and stared at the TV, still holding my hand. After a few minutes, probably convinced I was going to stay, he dropped my hand and smiled at me.

I sat quite a while, just "being there" with my boys.

The moment is seared into memory.

It was a sobering one, the perfect source for some mom guilt. Was I ignoring them? Had I forgotten that sometimes they just need Mama—not because something's wrong, not because they need help, but just because?

I was good at scolding myself for not having superhuman mom-vision. *Why didn't I realize this? Why didn't I see that coming?* The guilt kicked in because I thought I should know it all and be everything to my sons. Even while I worked. Maybe because I worked?

But that day, in the sitting, a lesson took root that I would learn repeatedly throughout my life.

I can't do it all or anticipate it all, as a mother or a professional. What I can do is let grace replace guilt, learn, and keep moving forward. I can talk to my kids about how hard it is to do two things at once. I can talk to them about God's amazing grace for all of us. I can make choices in the moment to prioritize instead of feel paralyzed.

The Bible tells us in 2 Corinthians that "My grace is sufficient for you, for my power is made perfect in weakness."

My sons need stronger hands than mine to hold. And what better way to lead them to God than to let him shine through my weakness. The realization that I couldn't do it all helped me depend more on my Source, and sharing that let the boys depend more on God too.

A call for Mom still comes today—just because. No crisis, no request for funds. Just because.

There are no longer TV trays and tubs of Cheerios. But the joy of resting with them, and in God, remains.

Reflections

In what areas of mothering am I hardest on myself? Do I feel extra pressure because I work outside the home, or because I don't?

9

Monkey Bars
and Cardboard Cars

God Is with Us . . . in Laughter and Play

Therefore, whoever takes the lowly position of
this child is the greatest in the kingdom of heaven.
And whoever welcomes one such child in my name
welcomes me.

Matthew 18:4–5

He was closer to two than to talking. That worried me
down deep, in that what-if place a mother keeps quiet.
But that night, he didn't need words.

I was doing the dinner dance, inhaling food while never
really touching fanny to chair while my little boys ate. I turned
back to them from the kitchen, and froze.

Little Luke had taken his fettuccine and lined up noodle
after noodle after noodle, hanging them off the table. *Dozens*

of noodles. The length of the table. Each strand perfectly equidistant from the next.

A dangling pasta rainbow.

It was God's reminder to me that he wasn't going to leave—in this case, leave Luke speechless. The boy obviously had plenty to communicate. A flood came *after* this rainbow, the spilled-milk kind.

I was busy getting the camera.

We have a choice each day whether to delight in our children's play or simply clean it up. Whether to join in or stop its progression. Whether to look deeper to see what they're saying even when they aren't yet saying. Not every mom is comfortable pretending to be Barbie, or shooting bad guys, or creating a hospital for stuffed animals. But play isn't just about silly voices, it's about hearing God's voice.

There is decidedly "a time to weep and a time to laugh, a time to mourn and a time to dance" (Eccles. 3:4). Laughter is mentioned in the Bible sometimes as derisive, but also as blessing and relief: "Blessed are you who weep now, for you will laugh" (Luke 6:21).

That's what a ninety-year-old Sarah did, when she was eavesdropping outside a tent and heard her hundred-year-old husband Abraham being told they would finally have a child.

"God has brought me laughter," she said, when that promise became reality (see Gen. 21:6). Abraham named that son Isaac, which means "he laughs."

Laughter downs defenses and lets in possibility.

Gritty kitchen floors and major work deadlines call out to us. Those are real demands and need attention. But "Unless the LORD builds the house, the builders labor in vain" (Ps. 127:1). As mothers we have to make sure our numerous priorities are lining up with what God wants for us. That can change in the time it takes someone to say, "Play-Doh, Mom?"

I think God wants us to truly know our children. Sometimes that is best done on your knees, at their eye level, wearing a ridiculous costume.

For a long time when I read of Jesus saying, "Let the little children come to me, and do not hinder them, for the kingdom of God belongs to such as these" (Mark 10:14), I thought simply of how sweet kids are. As an adult, I still love the verse but am convicted by it. Even those with the closest ties to Jesus, in this case his disciples, are mistakenly dismissing the touch of children.

How will they find their voice if we won't really listen to it?

Play isn't just about letting go of your inner grown-up. Sometimes it's just letting go. The endless questions, the sound effects, the toys-turned-projectiles, the role-playing, the book worn thin from repetition. Even when we aren't playing with them ourselves, we need to respect the way our kids are exploring the world.

And yes, sometimes even when we don't want to, we need to take a walk without having a destination. To see what our kids see in the clouds, and remind us all who created them. To bust a move, just because.

I often turn up music to lighten my post-dinner-cleanup mood, and when I do I always take a second to twirl a little boy. That won't scrape the buttered pasta off the table, but it reminds me what really matters.

There *is* a time to dance.

> Meet me in the clouds and on the playground,
>   Lord.
> Help unleash my grown-up spirit to imagine and
>   linger with my children.

Making the Lesson Stick

Julia Attaway

"For my thoughts are not your thoughts,
neither are your ways my ways,"
declares the LORD.

Isaiah 55:8

I'd collapsed into one of those instantaneous, inadvertent naps of the eighth month of pregnancy. Four-year-old Elizabeth awakened me, tugging on my arm. "Johnnie won't let me play with any of those sticky things!" she whined.

My eyelids flashed open as my brain scrambled to make sense of this news. *Sticky things? What sticky things?* I propelled my massive belly into the living room, where I beheld two-year-old John's latest project: a sofa entirely covered in sanitary pads. Much to Elizabeth's dismay, I burst into laughter.

Where does he get these ideas? At least this one was funny. Earlier in the week John had created a Van Gogh–like series of swirls on the living room carpet with the soil from our window plants. Before that it was the experiment with the confetti-like effect of rice cereal flakes (yes, half a box can cover a kitchen floor). And I won't go into detail about the sparks that flew when he figured out that the legs to the bathroom sink could be unscrewed and banged against our ancient enameled bathtub.

It was with good reason we'd given this child his own Dustbuster for Christmas.

As I settled wearily into a chair and sent John to get a trash bag, I sent up a quick prayer of thanks that today's mess didn't require a two-hour cleanup. But still I wondered how I could know my son so well and yet be so clueless about what went on in that little brain. I'd be cruising along, thinking I knew what he was doing—or perhaps more to the point, what *I* was doing—and then suddenly we were off-road again, bumping through territory I'd never imagined.

Would I ever figure him out?

I looked at my son's giggling, sandy-blond head as he made bunny ears for his sister out of a pair of sanitary napkins and knew I was asking the wrong question.

It wasn't my job to understand John's every thought, or to be able to predict his actions. My job was to love him. To teach him about God. To nurture his gifts and correct his faults. And yet that wasn't the whole of it. Whenever my jaw dropped or my temper flared, when I heard myself again say, "Lord, I just can't stand this!" I sensed there was more to motherhood than helping my child grow up. Two kids and another due soon, and I still hadn't figured it out.

The baby in my belly moved, stretching my skin to what felt like the breaking point. I shifted uncomfortably. As I watched John and Elizabeth make a silly game out of de-sticky-thing-ing the sofa, an odd thought came to mind. *Children are a gift because they highlight my weaknesses.*

John's never-ending stream of messy ideas put a spotlight on where my heart needed to change. It was as if God was gently saying, "Look, do you see how you must grow in patience?" or scolding, "Ahhh, but you *do* like to have things your way!" or reminding me, "See? Your love will grow when you learn to look from another perspective."

I closed my eyes to think this through. When I opened them my children were standing in front of me, laughing and sporting white, oblong beards. I grinned and gathered them into my arms, thanking God for the hard parts of motherhood and asking for help in seeing them as ways to draw closer to him.

Reflections

What parts of my children's play are hardest for me to allow, or to join them in? What might God be teaching me about myself through their silliness?

Spinning

Sharri Bockheim Steen

See what great love the Father has lavished on us,
that we should be called children of God! And
that is what we are!

1 John 3:1

The message from the teacher noted that I hadn't yet chaperoned any field trips. Would I like another opportunity before school ended?

It was a Mommy Guilt Moment.

Even though my schedule had been taken over by breast cancer–related doctor appointments, surgeries, and now chemotherapy, I took my parenting duties seriously. The kids' nursing home trip, though not the most exciting, was the only fit.

Our preschoolers and kindergarteners recited a poem, sang a song, and visited with residents. As the children dutifully gave out handmade cards and made shy conversation, four-year-old Anna found a clear space among the tables and wheelchairs, threw out her arms, and began to spin.

She spun with abandon. She laughed with delight, first turning one direction and then the other. She just kept spinning.

My inner parent vigilantly checked for sharp corners and other hazards. My inner chaperone sternly reminded me that I really ought to stop this inappropriate field trip behavior. But my inner chaperone is uncomfortable reprimanding other people's children. I looked around to see if a teacher or another parent was heading our direction. Nobody was.

And then I saw the residents' faces. They lit up brighter than they had during the recitations. Some laughed aloud. They seemed to find more delight in a child just being a child than in her dispatched duties. An unexpected moment of pure joy.

I loosened up too and enjoyed my time all the more.

Several days later I started my next chemotherapy round. Again would come debilitating fatigue and feelings of failure from my inability to "do." I remembered Anna's moment. And I saw both of us through God's eyes.

We feel relief when our children reach a new milestone: rolling over or using the potty. We feel pride in their accomplishments: learning to write or draw a recognizable rocket or cat. But we feel pure delight in watching them be children: discovering, playing, and doing any silly, spontaneous thing that mysteriously enters their minds. How I delight in overhearing my daughter tell her stuffed animals a story or in seeing her run her fastest across the lawn for no particular reason.

God feels that way about us. He delights in us simply for being his children. In this driven world, we often feel our value comes from performance or success: as wives or mothers, in vocations or volunteerism, in our own minds or in the public eye. We might fail to be the mother we pictured ourselves to be, we might lose a job, we might be sidelined by illness or injury.

We might end up someday like those nursing home residents, segregated from the world and what seem to be any and all valuable roles.

But our value does not come from our own spinning from task to task, but in simply being children of God. We did nothing to deserve it and need not do anything to prove our worth. We are much, much more than products of our productivity. We are God's beloved daughters, his sources of delight.

I needed to be reminded of this every time the effects of chemotherapy prevent me from checking things off my chronically overambitious to-do list. I can still delight in the play of my children, though I struggle with not being productive. That's when I need to remember that, just as the nursing home residents delighted in Anna, God delights in me.

Not because of my dispatched duties, but simply because I am his child.

Reflections

Does my sense of what must be done interfere with my ability to just "be" with my family? How can I work to change that?

Being Needled

Gina Kell Spehn

Even in laughter the heart may ache,
and rejoicing may end in grief.

Proverbs 14:13

I was standing at the kitchen sink peeling potatoes for Thanksgiving dinner; our house was bustling with family and an abundance of blessings. I couldn't think of one thing to want for, and I was reminded of the privilege and responsibility that come with being given so much.

In that moment I decided to let down my guard and listen to some Christmas music.

Every year a local radio station begins playing Christmas music shortly after Halloween. I've made it known I despise this annual tradition. I resent being beaten into "holiday season submission" (not Christmas) by a radio station, so I remove it from my preset dial for two months every year.

Some are convinced that I shun the season because my husband died on Christmas Day. While that does influence my attitude, in reality my resistance to this season has slowly evolved over many years.

I admit I have allowed a series of tragedies to strip away my joy. I really don't want to be told that "It's the Most Wonderful Time of the Year" when it simply doesn't feel that way. I've become apathetic about pulling out bins of decorations, and I don't want to put up a tree that will inevitably rain pine needles for four weeks and damage ornaments and carpet when it falls over, fully decorated, as it has every year for the last three. The good news is that we do laugh hysterically about it every year.

In my kitchen, while most of the family was in the basement watching football, I continued peeling and chopping. The first song to come on the radio was, of course, "It's the Most Wonderful Time of the Year." I laughed out loud. It was either a cruel joke or a tailor-made lighten-up-already message just for me.

But "O Holy Night" was next. Tears began to flow. My mind was flooded with joyful and painful memories of years past. I suddenly understood why my defenses are so high this time of year. Vulnerability. If I let down my guard, I risked opening myself up to pain. I have done my best to keep the holiday season at bay because it is filled with vivid remembrances that are equally heartwarming and heartbreaking.

I deeply desire to live my life in submission to Christ. Although I fail miserably at times, my heart is humbly aware of the gift of his birth, life, and death. So often my reality does not align with my theology. I can easily taint the moment I'm in by lamenting what was, what is, or even what has never been. By choosing to turn off the music or keep the Christmas bins in storage, I was shortchanging my relationship with my kids, family, friends, and most of all, Jesus.

Whether in the midst of the holy season or on a random Tuesday in June, moms have struggles that can prevent us from engaging in a lighthearted way with family or even God.

Tucking away laughter and play is not a means of guarding the heart. In fact, the opposite is true. Although I still prefer not to hear Andy Williams crooning before I've had a chance to put away the Halloween costumes, Christmas is for celebrating . . . every day.

I overflow with gratitude for all that has been given, including that which has also been taken away.

Allowing my pain to stifle my appreciation for God's tender mercies is a symptom of my unbelief, and I am thankful for his forgiveness. I love the Lord's sense of humor, gently needling me with whimsical Christmas songs to shake me out of my malaise and draw me closer to him.

Bring on the tree.

Reflections

Am I shutting my heart off to God's blessings and my children's joy by guarding my heart in some way?

Today I Was a Zebra

Ann Kronwald

You must observe my Sabbaths. This will be a sign
between me and you for the generations to come,
so you may know that I am the LORD, who makes
you holy.

Exodus 31:13

Today I was a zebra. My best four-year-old pal, Jack, was
a lion. He roared and chased. I galloped and screamed.
As I maneuvered around the lawn to evade his fierce grasp, I
could not stifle my laughter. This was actually fun, even though
Jack needed to reprimand me because zebras don't scream.

While little Emma and James looked on, my wee lion
finally overtook his prey, and we tumbled together in the
grass. Emma noticed a break in the action and quickly convinced Jack to be a car with her. So, of course, James and I
plopped down on top of their wiggly bodies. As I grinned
and "gunned" my engine, the simple pleasure of the moment
overwhelmed me.

Yes, this was fun. *Why don't I play more often? When did
I start equating godliness with completing my to-do list?* I
was sad to think how often my efficient and fast-paced life
had elbowed out silliness and imagination. In my busyness,
I had allowed organization and accomplishment to crowd
out this important and affectionate play.

When King David brought the ark of God back to Jerusalem, he ended his work with shouting, trumpet playing,

173

dancing, leaping, offerings, and great joy. In his wife's eyes, he appeared foolish. But David defended the importance of his celebration as something special for the Lord and said, "Therefore will I play before the LORD" (2 Sam. 6:21 KJV).

I know work is a blessing from God, something he gifts to us. I love completing a task, whether it is matching all the socks, packing the final lunchbox, or handing the last kid in the church nursery back to their parents. There is something inherently satisfying in the work we accomplish. But God established rest from work as well.

After the "work" of creation, God rested on the seventh day. He set apart, or sanctified, a day for rest. God told the nation of Israel to regularly observe his Sabbath rest to help them understand that God, not their work, set them apart and made them special to him. In fact, God named himself *Jehovah Mekoddishkem*, "the LORD who sanctifies you." He connected this name to the Sabbath rest, so that every time we rest from our work, we will remember that God is the sanctifier, not our accomplishments, whether spectacular or mundane.

So I am learning to thank God for his presence in my play. His gentle prodding for me to take a break from my work and play a bit is a nudge to enjoy his creation, to build relationships, and to listen to his voice. When I take time to tumble with my favorite toddlers, I don't need to count the minutes ticking off the clock as wasted.

Even in play, *Jehovah Mekoddishkem* is at work making me perfect for the roles he has for me.

My eternal value is not in my work. It is not even in my rest or play. It lies in God alone. So with great delight, I'll be a zebra and feel God's presence there.

Reflections

Do I find it hard to stop and play? Do I value rest or put more stock in "the rest"?

Laugh

Amy Storms

The cheerful heart has a continual feast.

Proverbs 15:15

When I was young, my grandpa and I played a silly game. Over and over again, we'd take turns saying "ha" to each other, adding another "ha" with every turn.

"Ha," Grandpa would start.

"Ha ha," I'd reply.

"Ha ha ha."

And on and on, until one of us would finally erupt into real laughter. We called our game, quite creatively, "Laugh." The object of Laugh was to go the longest without cracking up. I never made it past a string of six.

"Ha ha ha ha ha ha . . ." and we'd dissolve into a laughing fit.

A simple game, filled with precious memories for me. Grandpa had cancer, and he died when I was still in grade school. We played Laugh as he sat in his recliner after cancer treatments. We played Laugh when he was too sick to do anything else. We played Laugh because, though faced with illness and pain and the prospect of not watching his grandchildren grow up, Grandpa had the hope of heaven. He still had the joy to laugh.

A few years ago, I asked my three kids what things they most enjoy doing together as a family. I anticipated they'd say amusement parks, restaurants, and trips. I wasn't prepared for their answers.

"Taking hikes!" said my son Nathan.

"Playing UNO!" Anne chimed in.

"When we all go for walks!" answered Molly.

My kids prefer UNO to Chuck E. Cheese? They'd rather go on a hike than to Disneyland? They asked for togetherness, for time, for fun. Ultimately, they value the same thing I treasured with my grandpa: the simple gift of laughter.

Laughter gives life. When our family laughs together, we make memories, and our hearts are bound by joy. Laughter doesn't deny the hardships and struggles. Like Grandpa, we face illness and pain and an unknown future. And yet, because of Jesus, we can still laugh. Laughter lightens the load.

Laughter makes memories. When they're grown, I want Nathan, Anne, and Molly to remember our home as a place that rang with laughter. I want them to recall the mealtimes when our sides ached, not from too much food, but from too much fun. I want them to know how much their dad and I simply enjoyed them.

"You make me laugh," we tell them. "You bring me joy."

But laughter also takes time. Maybe that's why we don't always prioritize it as we should. Amusement park fun is easy enough to contrive, but true laughter needs time and intention. Life-giving laughter happens when we linger around the family dinner table, or spend a few extra minutes at bedtime each night, or turn off the TV and snuggle on the couch. Memory-making laughter happens in relationships, and relationships take time.

For the family who laughs together, it's all the pleasure of Thanksgiving dinner without all the prep and cleanup. Every day is a celebration, regardless of the circumstances.

Every day is life-giving and memory-making in a home filled with laughter.

Reflections

What truly makes my family laugh? Have I considered that laughter is one of God's gifts and one he wants me to open regularly?

10

Nourishment

God Is with Us . . . and Provides

And my God will meet all your needs according to the riches of his glory in Christ Jesus.

Philippians 4:19

I was shaking mad. The kind of mad that scares a mom. They weren't listening. I was yelling.

It was week three alone with my three young sons in a family beach condo, connected by computer to my husband three states away as he worked a new assignment and tried to find us a new home. *The beach*—yes, I know. What could possibly be the problem?

I felt like a crumpled can of days-old soda. My fizz was gone. The shiny attitude of adventure I'd left our home of eight years with was in dire need of recycling.

I didn't know what I needed, besides a home. I was just so empty.

• We all know the mothering potholes of patience, sleep, money, creative ideas, and self-confidence. We can feel empty in those areas—as in vacant. The other synonym strain for *empty* is empty as in meaningless, purposeless, and pointless.

Big difference. But the same God exists over a broken budget and a broken spirit. He is a God who provides. "Blessed are the poor in spirit, for theirs is the kingdom of heaven. Blessed are those who mourn, for they will be comforted" (Matt. 5:3–4).

We are *not* told, "Blessed are those who want new shoes, for they will be sent an anonymous gift card in the mail." Too often we see what we don't have, instead of what we do. Too often our idea of provision is getting what we want, instead of accepting what God wants to give us.

That summer I wanted out of that condo. What he wanted for me was right there in it.

I love the story in the Bible of how God provided for the prophet Elijah. After he commanded a punitive, three-year drought, there was famine. God told his faithful servant to travel near to the Jordan and said to him, "You will drink from the brook, and I have directed the ravens to supply you with food there" (1 Kings 17:4).

Ravens are birds of prey and are certainly not known for sharing. A very unlikely source of provision. So was a dried-up brook. Likewise, we are being given to, even when it seems like the world (or the job of mothering) is only taking from us.

When Abraham was asked to sacrifice his son Isaac to God, and was an obedient strike away from doing so, an angelic voice was sent to halt the bloodshed and deliver a promise of great blessing.

"So Abraham called that place The LORD Will Provide. And to this day it is said, 'On the mountain of the LORD it will be provided'" (Gen. 22:14).

Trusting on the mountain, or in the valley, is difficult. God doesn't always provide the resolution of a crisis in relationships or finances or health the way we'd like. Many times we don't provide the faithfulness I'm sure *he'd* like. In life's storms we sometimes find safe harbor and don't credit him. Other times we stagger through the current and rage at him. I like to imagine he sees each of us in neon rain gear—never out of his sight.

That long, hot summer, God provided a church in a converted movie theater whose Hawaiian-shirted congregation lifted my spirits so I could hold on, sunscreen, and safety-monitor for a few more days. He provided some inspiration for non-beach activities, and a visiting family that took interest in us. He provided someone to stop and help when my sweltering car's battery died.

The three-hour Wal-Mart wait for a new battery proved one of the longest and, with toy bribes, most expensive days we had. I bought a gaudy crab Christmas ornament to commemorate the experience. God also provided me with a sense of humor.

Ultimately our move, thirteen house offers later, resulted in a home that led us to this life and these friends. To this day I'm embarrassed by my trapped-in-the-tropics blowups at the children I prayed so desperately for and God so faithfully provided.

Now when we go to the beach, I always enter with a smiling, respectful nod to what happened there. Perhaps we need to name all our homes "that place the Lord will provide."

> *Lord you have nourished me and I still hunger.*
> *Help me trust that you will always give me what*
> *I need.*

You Are Enough

Carol Kuykendall

Give your entire attention to what God is doing
right now, and don't get worked up about what
may or may not happen tomorrow. God will help
you deal with whatever hard things come up when
the time comes.

Matthew 6:34 Message

My daughter Kendall and I flew from California to Colorado with her two-year-old son Tennyson. Flying with a preschooler is one of her most feared challenges, but this was a necessary trip.

"I still have post-traumatic stress disorder from our last flight," she told me nervously as we waited to board the plane. I remembered her vow never to fly with him again after that nightmare cry-a-thon. "He's going on no nap, a little sugar, and still hates being confined to small spaces," she said, summarizing the circumstances that might create another perfect storm of trouble.

I could feel Kendall's anxiety as we finally boarded. She smiled at the passengers around us, as if to apologize in advance that they had drawn the unlucky assignment of sitting near a potential crier for the next two hours.

Kendall came prepared with plenty of provisions, and for the first hour Tennyson seemed fine with both of us keeping him entertained. We read books, played games, put the tray table down, then up. Put the window shade up, then down.

He ate Goldfish, Lightning McQueen fruit snacks, and a semi-cold cheeseburger. But then suddenly, he was done. And he told us so.

Uh-oh.

He slithered out of his seat onto the floor. Kendall scooped him up and he began crying. She lifted him onto her lap and tenderly tried to comfort him, snuggling his head under her chin. But he cried louder. And then began coughing, and we both knew what might come next: the gag reflex.

Sure enough.

In slow motion, with small heaving sounds, he began to throw up . . . all over Kendall. It seeped down inside her shirt and pooled into her lap. Frantically, I began searching for a bag in the seat pocket in front of me and found a couple of small napkins, but the mess was already made. I expected Kendall to have her own meltdown. She didn't.

She calmly continued to comfort Tennyson and then made a dabbing attempt to clean them both up, not very successfully, with the napkins plus the small wad of tissues I found in my purse.

Kendall was doing what she assumed a mom had to do. But as her mom, I saw something much more sacred. Here was my daughter, who used to have a dramatic aversion to anything stinky or sticky touching her skin when she was Tennyson's age. Toilet water or another child's dirty diaper sent her shrieking the other way. When she was about ten and had to help her older sister clean manure out of the horse stalls, she always wore high boots and soaked two pieces of tissue with perfume and stuck them up her nose. She couldn't tolerate the smell. But the worst was vomit. Whenever she caught a whiff of a sibling's throw-up, she'd always say she too was going to puke.

I sat in my seat, watching her gently rock Tennyson, oblivious to other passengers around her or the stinky mess she was wearing. And I saw the work of God's hand: how he allows little girls like her to be silly, shrieking, playful children. But when they grow up and become mothers, he transforms and feeds and sustains them with exactly what they need to carry out the call to mothering. In messy moments like this, sitting in seat 16A. And in so many other yucky, open-to-public-scrutiny moments.

He pours into mothers as they pour into their children, making them enough. Because he is enough.

A plane trip always makes me feel closer to God in the sky above the clouds. I breathed my own prayer of gratitude for this visual reminder of his tender provisions.

Reflections

When I feel like crumbling, what keeps it from happening? How can I keep track of these moments to remind myself of God's provision and see myself grow as a mom?

Running on Empty

Rachel Jankovic

Give, and it will be given to you. A good measure,
pressed down, shaken together and running over,
will be poured into your lap. For with the measure
you use, it will be measured to you.

Luke 6:38

As any mother of young children knows, energy is a precious commodity. Most little children have a limitless supply of it, and most mothers don't.

Without energy, even the simplest things become overwhelming. Buckling children into the car. Nursing a baby while the toddler dumps Legos. Needing to make dinner when you want to take a nap.

I cannot count the times when the days seemed to lay out before me like a Nebraska highway but my gas gauge was already pointing straight to empty. Sometimes you feel you can even see a sign that says, "Next gas station: sometime tonight, after dinner, maybe."

The worst of it is you really want to do the work. You really want to be able to make it to the grocery store, clean the house, and have happy and cared-for children. You want to watch the highway flying past, feel the warm wind in your hair. But you look at your energy level, and you look at the day before you, and you simply *know* it cannot be done.

I clearly remember a phase in my life when my twins were babies and my older two girls were pretty much toddlers. Waking up from a busy night with babies to a busy day with toddlers *and* babies was frequently a discouraging and overwhelming thing. I just knew I didn't have what the day would take.

And then I would remember that wonderful story of the widow and her oil (see 2 Kings 4). I didn't need to have energy. God wasn't asking me to give what I had enough of. He was asking me to give what I didn't have enough of. Like he had asked the widow who was down to the last drops of oil, he was asking me to pour.

> Pour it into this vessel, these children.
> Give my empty cruet of oil, and He would fill it.
> But He would only fill it as I poured.
> Pour and it will keep coming.
> Drive, and the car will not stop.

But if I worried about it, treasured that little bit of leftover oil . . . if I parked on the side of the highway and cried about it . . . if I said I could not give any away because there was only enough for me, then there would be no oil, there would be no peace, there would be no progress.

But if I looked to the Lord, and if I said, "Lord, give to me what you want me to give. I will pour, and I know that you will fill," he always did.

Although I have had many opportunities to learn this lesson and many days where I have been overwhelmed first by my work, and then by his mercy to me in it, I still have much to learn. I still need to greet that feeling with faith, with comfort in his care.

This headache, this pile of work to do, this little batch of children who need my care, this house that is feeling less than homey—these are my vessels.

They are empty, and the Lord has told me to pour. I look at my insufficiency, I look at the work, and I need to laugh.

Laugh, because I know what God will do.
Pour, because I believe him.
Fill, because he is true to his promise.

Reflections

What do I turn to when I'm feeling emptied out by mother-hood? Will that work for me in the long run?

The Deeper Waters

Leeana Tankersley

> When you go through deep waters,
> I will be with you.
>
> Isaiah 43:2 NLT

I was nine weeks pregnant, and when I went in for the first ultrasound, the doctor couldn't find a heartbeat.

Amidst this loss, my husband Steve, our twins, and I were waiting for his next set of orders with the navy. We had been told that he might be going overseas *and* that he might be staying in San Diego at his current job. Back and forth. Back and forth. No clarity in sight.

Finally, orders came: to the middle eastern country of Bahrain. Because of violent demonstrations in the region, we were told we might not be allowed to go with him. We were facing a year of separation.

For weeks we sat in the unknown, our future as an intact family very unclear.

I was trying to process the miscarriage. I was trying my very best to take care of my amazing twins and not give in to the temptation to let Curious George raise them.

That entire season was categorized by a deep silence, as though I had no words for any of these events. I felt silence around my miscarriage. I was in shock for so long—shocked that I got pregnant in the first place and then shocked that the pregnancy was snatched away so abruptly.

I felt as though something inside me had been muted.

And as we sat and waited for the final outcome with the navy and anticipated Steve's departure, I truly felt silent. The pleasantries and "it could be so much worse," and "God will sustain us," and "He has a plan" didn't even begin to put words to the hollow place deep inside me.

As much as I wanted to run from the pain, I knew it would still be there. Unattended pain is toxic. I had to do the thing that seemed most counterintuitive. I had to reach into the discomfort.

A part of me would rather numb out in front of reruns of *The Real Housewives of Some County*, but I know that disconnecting ultimately leads to death. Soul death. Instead, I had to move toward the deeper waters.

I believe attending to the deeper waters is holy work, and it was Jesus's invitation to me. He didn't love me by rescuing me from the swirling circumstances, which I would have likely preferred.

He loved me by buoying me within the current.

As I admitted my need to him, he answered. Often, he answered in the most unexpectedly practical ways: a meal at my door, a playdate for my kids, an understanding email.

Time after time in Scripture, Jesus asks someone to confront the ache. To the woman at the well he asks, "Do you want living water?" To the man at the pool in Bethesda he asks, "Do you want to get well?" To the Pharisees he asks, "Why do you break the command of God for the sake of your tradition?"

To his followers he asks, "What good would it be for someone to gain the whole world yet forfeit their soul?"

To the disciples, as he washes their feet, he asks, "Do you realize what I have done for you?"

We must allow Christ to take us into the depth of the matter. When we live this way, we are put in touch with our great need and also with Christ's ministering presence.

189

This is not the presence we know about cognitively. This is not the presence we believe to be there in theory. This is the presence we experience.

When we have the courage to venture down into that silent ache, to sit in it, we find Christ there.

Reflections

Do I tend to run away from sadness or run into it? What would I imagine Jesus saying to me about the current state of my heart?

Pruning Me

Kim Hill

Though he may stumble, he will not fall,
    for the LORD upholds him with his hand.

Psalm 37:24

A few days before September 11, 2001, I became a single mom of my two boys, ages four and seven.

As my own personal tragedy fell against the backdrop of a much larger national tragedy, I was completely overwhelmed. I didn't know if I would have a job after my divorce, having worked as a worship leader for conservative Christian ministries. Many well-meaning friends encouraged me to think of a new career.

Amid all the changes I was facing as a single mom, I'd just moved from a beautiful custom home, where I had designed and decorated everything, into a small cottage built in the 1930s.

God's promise in Psalm 34:18 to be "close to the brokenhearted and [save] those who are crushed in spirit" became my hope and my reality.

Every night the boys asked very hard questions. I didn't have all the answers. But the Lord quickly and graciously gave me answers far beyond what I could've thought of on my own. It was truly as if one by one he dropped them into my brain and heart, straight from heaven.

I began to experience God as literally the Provider of every answer I needed during that season. He was truly the "husband to the husbandless and the Father to the fatherless" in my little "peace house," as we affectionately called our little cottage.

Each day I realized more and more that clinging to the Lord as my provider, *Jehovah Jireh* (see Gen. 22:14), meant relying on him to provide for me both financially and emotionally. I knew God wasn't a big vending machine, but he gave gifts that let us know he saw, he cared, he was with us, and he knew the secrets of our hearts.

Some of those gifts were tangible, some intangible. I needed strength for my boys and myself each day. He provided for me in ways I hadn't even thought of before this valley in my life—like the neighbor who taught my son to tie a tie for his Christmas program.

One day I had an estimate done for cutting down a few trees to build a carport. I was disappointed that it was far beyond my budget; the tree company wanting $2,000 to take down just the biggest tree I needed removed.

A few days later, Nashville Electric crewmen arrived, un-announced. They cut down all of the trees I needed removed because they were too close to the power line—including the $2,000 tree. Not only did they cut them down, but they also planted ten Bradford pear trees in my yard and allowed me to choose where to place them.

All this, in exchange for a six-pack of Coke. They said they couldn't take what money I tried to offer. I was in shock.

A few days later I talked with a neighbor who showed me her backyard and bemoaned the fact that she'd had to pay thousands of dollars to have trees removed. I had assumed the Nashville Electric crew did hers for free as well. But no one else on our street had the "free service." My neighbor thought maybe my guys were really angels in disguise.

I wrestled for years with my circumstances, not wanting this for my life or my boys. But I knew I had in them what mattered most, and as we found a place to heal we also found the chance to become more dependent on God in all ways.

The night of the tree removal, I relayed the story of God's amazing provision to my boys and was again reminded that he truly is the God who sees (see Gen. 16:13). His promise to provide "everything we need for a godly life" (2 Pet. 1:3) goes beyond what we can imagine.

Reflections

Does my idea of what I need often seem at odds with what I'm given? How do my material circumstances affect my view of God and his provision?

Forever Father

Kelly Combs

> Though my father and mother forsake me,
> the LORD will receive me.
>
> Psalm 27:10

W ho is your forever mommy?"

Somehow my preschooler's question caught me off guard as I tucked her into bed. We had been reading *Love You Forever*, a children's book about a mommy who promised to love her son forever, and even when she was very old she still sang about her love to him. After we finished the story, I told my daughter I was her "forever mommy" and would love her always.

So her question was a natural response to the story. *Who was my forever mommy?*

"My mom is called Nene, but you don't know her," I told her. "Now go to sleep." And with her question answered, she stuck her thumb into her mouth and closed her eyes.

I was relieved she hadn't pursued the questioning, but I knew that day would come. What would I tell her? My "forever mommy" didn't love me forever. Or perhaps she did, but her mental illness and alcohol abuse were more of a constant in our relationship than the outward showing of her love. I tried to stay in a relationship with her, but I could not.

So I do not have a forever mommy in my life. It's hard for me to admit that, because well-meaning people often tell me if I would just try harder, pray more, or be a better daughter, I could have a relationship with my mom. They haven't experienced the years of emotional abuse that I have. They don't know that the reason I ended the relationship was not because she hurt me, but because when I saw the first glimmer of that hurt in my older daughter's eyes, I realized that if I wasn't strong enough to end the relationship for me, I would for my child.

Still, I have longed for a "forever mommy," a mom to comfort me when I am feeling discouraged, a mom to be a grandma to my kids when I need a break, a mom to guide me through those tough parenting moments. I know there are other mothers, like me, who long for their own mothers to be an active part of their lives. But we do have a *forever father*, a heavenly Father who loves us and is with us every step of our parenting journey.

When we need comfort, our forever father tells us, "As a mother comforts a child, so will I comfort you" (Isa. 66:13).

When we are tired and need a break, our forever father says, "Come to me, all you who are weary and burdened, and I will give you rest" (Matt. 11:28).

When we need guidance, our forever father declares that his Word is "a lamp for [your] feet, a light on [your] path" (Ps. 119:105).

When we need parenting direction, our forever father informs us not to exasperate our children; instead, "bring them up in the training and instruction of the Lord" (Eph. 6:4).

Mothering without a mother to look to has been tough at times, but when I look at my forever father, I see such a model of grace, mercy, discipline—and most of all love—that I know I'm not alone.

God didn't just provide me himself and his Word; now I am able to see other women he placed in my life at just the right time. My grandmother, special teachers, a friend's mom, and my mother-in-law provide good role models for my parenting.

So I didn't learn how to be a mom from my mom, but from God my Father. The best part about this Father is that he gave me *eternal* life. He will truly love me . . . forever.

Reflections

How does my relationship with my own parents influence the kind of parent I am? Have I asked God to fill any gaps?

Contributors

Jenne Acevedo is a writer, speaker, and substitute teacher. She lives in Chandler, Arizona, with her husband and three children. She is an avid reader who loves studying God's Word, traveling, and entertaining in her home. Encouraging women to find their worth and hope in Christ is her passion. www.jenneacevedo.com.

Julia Attaway is a freelance writer and mother of five. She lives in New York City, where she homeschools three of her children. A regular contributor to *Daily Guideposts*, Julia recently edited *Daily Guideposts: Your First Year of Motherhood*, a devotional book for new moms.

Rachel Swenson Balducci is married to Paul, and they parent five lively boys and one precious daughter. A columnist for the *Southern Cross*, she writes at Testosterhome.net and at *Faith and Family Live!* She is author of *How Do You Tuck in a Superhero and Other Delightful Mysteries of Raising Boys* (Revell, 2010).

Tracey Bianchi is a mother of three completely messy preschoolers. She is the author of the 2012 MOPS theme book *Mom Connection: Creating Vibrant Relationships in the Midst of Motherhood*, a speaker and writer, and a founding member of Redbud Writers Guild. She and her husband make their home in the Chicago suburbs. http://traceybianchi.com.

Mary Ellen Blatchford was a pastor's wife for twenty years until her husband's sudden death. A mother of four, she remarried a widower and has added the blessing of two stepchildren to her life. Cherishing family and helping others through grief and loss, Mary Ellen also uses her voice of experience to belt out praise music.

Writer and speaker **Alicia Bruxvoort** is the mother of five children ages three to thirteen. Her minivan is at capacity, but she wants a soul filled to the brim too, and blogs about that at *The Overflow*. www.aliciabrux voort.net.

Suanne Camfield is blog manager for *FullFill* magazine, writer, speaker, and cofounder of Redbud Writers Guild. She is married to Eric and has two elementary-aged children. She works for InterVarsity Press, floats ungracefully between work and parenting, and (much to her dismay) finds it impossible to read on a treadmill. She blogs at www.suannecamfield. wordpress.com.

Kelly Combs is an over-caffeinated and under-compensated stay-at-home mom who writes and lives in Virginia. Her daughters are now eight and twelve, but Kelly remembers a time when wisdom gleaned from her MOPS group stood in for her own mother. Visit her at www.kellycombs.com.

Presidential historian **Jane Hampton Cook** has written six books, including *What Does the President Look Like?* and *The Faith of America's First Ladies*. A mother of two young children, she is a MOPS speaker in Virginia (www.janecook.com) and a frequent guest on the FOX News channel.

Michele Cushatt is a speaker and author who writes in the tension between authentic faith and real life. Knowing every beautiful story begins with a rough first draft, Michele encourages others to live courageously, even when life is imperfect. She lives in Colorado with her husband and their three teenage boys.

Cindy Dagnan is an incredibly grateful and chronically sleepy wife and mother of four daughters ages ten to twenty. She blogs at www.cindy dagnan.com; writes *Responder Wife* for those married to first responders at www.responderlife.com; and writes on spiritual legacies for *Heritage Builders*.

Hayley DiMarco is the author of more than thirty books, of which twenty are bestsellers, six are Christian Book Award finalists, and two are winners (2007 and 2010). But her biggest accomplishment is as a mother; she and her daughter have survived and thrived together for six years. The DiMarco family resides just outside Nashville, Tennessee.

Elizabeth Esther is a married mother of five, a columnist, and a blogger. She lives in Southern California with her family and Darby the Diva Dog.

She enjoys walking on the beach, reading, cooking big Sunday Suppers, and laughing. You can read more of her musings at www.ElizabethEsther.com.

Jennifer Grant is an author and journalist who often writes about family life. She lives outside Chicago with her husband and four children. Author of the memoir *Love You More: The Divine Surprise of Adopting My Daughter*, Jennifer is a founding member of Redbud Writers Guild. Find her online at jennifergrant.com.

Laura Lee Groves is the mother of four redheaded sons. Reflecting on the days of a full and rather crazy nest, she uses her book, *I'm Outnumbered! One Mom's Lessons in the Lively Art of Raising Boys* (Kregel, 2010), and her blog, www.OutnumberedMom.com, to encourage and inspire other moms.

Carey Haivala is a mother of two and a television reporter. Her challenging journey through loss and toward motherhood propelled her to write *The Living Womb*. www.livingwomb.com.

Kimberly Henderson is a writer who lives in upstate South Carolina. She and her husband are raising three giggly girls and one lively schnauzer. Prayer, coffee, and the Word of God are some of her favorite parts of her day.

Amy Henry is a mom to six children ages seven to seventeen who always eat the Little Debbie oatmeal pies before she can get to them. She blogs about faith and parenting at www.wholemama.com.

Kim Hill has been a single mother for more than a decade to Graham and Benji and has been recording Christian music for twenty-three years. The Grammy nominee, Dove award–winner, and popular conference worship leader still claims her boys, now nineteen and fifteen, as her greatest accomplishments, bar none! www.KimHillmusic.com.

Lisa Howell raises Taylor and Katelyn with husband Brandon in Denver, where the purple mountains' majesty reminds them daily of God's presence and power. She credits MOPS for helping keep her family Christ-focused, helping her keep her mom-sanity, and bringing beautiful women like Kyndall into her life.

Beverly Hudson raised two sons who became US Marines. This time she's helping raise granddaughter Addy Grace each week, while her dad, an Iraq War veteran, earns his degree and her mom works full-time. Beverly and her husband of thirty-five years live in Pearland, Texas, in gratitude for God's provision.

Rachel Jankovic is a stay-at-home mother to five busy and hilarious children under seven, including twins. She is the author of *Loving the Little Years: Motherhood in the Trenches* and blogs at *Femina*. For obvious reasons, mothering little ones is a topic close to her heart.

Sue Jeantheau is a wife, a mother of two girls ages eight and thirteen, and a MOPS-affiliated woman of eleven years with the chapter at New Hanover Presbyterian Church in Mechanicsville, Virginia. No matter how the day has gone, she sweeps well at night.

Keri Wyatt Kent is the author of nine books that help people slow down, listen to God, and connect intimately with him. When she's not speaking or leading retreats, she's writing for several online outlets, including www. BuildingChurchLeaders.com. A founding member of Redbud Writers Guild, Keri lives with husband Scot and their teenage son and daughter in the Chicago area. www.KeriWyattKent.com.

Ann Kronwald writes and teaches women's Bible studies in Chandler, Arizona, where she lives and works with her husband David. They have four grown children and seven grandchildren. Ann enjoys writing about the names of God at www.HisNameMyPurpose.com.

Alexandra Kuykendall is now mom to four girls ages ten to one. When she is not locked in the bathroom or hiding from squirt-gun bandits, she serves as editor of Mom and Leader Content for MOPS International. You can connect with her on Twitter @alex_kuykendall.

Carol Kuykendall is a consulting editor and columnist for *MomSense* magazine and the author of many books about families and mothering. She's "Oma" to nine grandchildren and loves watching her children raise their children. She recently helped create and launch Stories, a ministry for women in her community. She and husband Lynn live in Boulder, Colorado.

Ashley Larkin is mom to three girls under ten and wife to Michael. She moves daily among the worlds of tetherball, toenail painting, and tea parties, often realizing she's forgotten to put away the laundry. Ashley is continually challenged to serve in joyful humility. Read more at ashley mlarkin.com.

Helen Lee is the author of *The Missional Mom: Living with Purpose in the Home and the World* and cofounder of Redbud Writers Guild. She lives in the Chicago area with husband Brian and three boys under nine, whom she attempts to homeschool when she is not dismantling laundry sculptures.

Kathi Lipp is mom and stepmom to four kids (most of whom are out of the house, and one who is just a little too comfortable there). While doing laundry, Kathi writes books for wives and moms. You can find more of Kathi's mom-musings at www.kathilipp.com.

Nancy Mendez is a New Orleans native who grew up on gumbo, beignets, and café au lait. She is discovering the culinary delights of Houston along with her husband of eleven years, Luis, and children, Oliver, age eight, and Vivian, age three. She is a proud alumnus of the West University Baptist MOPS group.

Shannon Milholland is the mother of four daughters ages toddler to teenager. She finds joy among piles of laundry and miles of carpools, and delights in helping other women find this place of contentment in life. Read more at shannonmilholland.blogspot.com.

Amy Parham was a contestant on NBC's *The Biggest Loser*. She authored *Ten Lessons from a Former Fat Girl* and coauthored *The 90-Day Fitness Challenge* and *The Amazing Fitness Adventure for Your Kids* with her husband Phillip. They live with sons Austin, Pearson, and Rhett in Simpsonville, South Carolina.

Michelle Rahn is mother to two, grandmother to five, former teacher to hundreds, and Ms. Senior America 2004. She's a professional speaker and MOPS Mentor in Colorado, having prayed with many women yearning for their husbands to come to know God, or at least come to church. Hers now does.

Caryn Rivadeneira is a writer, speaker, and founding member and managing partner of Redbud Writers Guild. She's the author of *Grumble Hallelujah: Learning to Love Your Life Even When It Lets You Down* (Tyndale, 2011) and *Mama's Got a Fake I.D.: How to Reveal the Real You Behind All That Mom*. Caryn lives with her husband, three kids, and one pit bull in the suburbs of Chicago.

Nicole Russell is a mother of three under age six, and has written for *Parents*, *Parenting*, and *Christianity Today*. She will forever be a foodie, but treasures Slurpees with her kids just as much.

Jennifer Sammons is the mother of four: Sawyer, Brooklyn, Annabelle, and Sarah Beth. She now spends her evenings as a chauffeur to practices and games, and has recently taught the children to clean toilets. The only recurring poop spectacle is *outside* her house, from her dog, Bear. Her son is in charge of shoveling.

Karen Halvorsen Schreck is a writer, teacher, and founding member of Redbud Writers Guild. She's the author of the award-winning children's book *Lucy's Family Tree* (Tilbury House) and the young adult novel *Dream Journal* (Hyperion). Her next novel, *Hold Me Forever* (Sourcebooks), is due out in 2012. She lives with her family outside of Chicago.

Gina Kell Spehn is mother to five, coauthor of *The Color of Rain* (Zondervan 2011), and director of New Day Foundation for Families. After losing her first husband to cancer, she married Michael, who lost his first wife to cancer. They host a weekly radio show and began the Forward Through Faith ministry. Visit www.MichaelandGina.com.

Sharri Bockheim Steen answers to "Mom" full-time when addressed by her children, ages seven and nine, and to "Dr. Steen" part-time when addressed by pharmaceutical clients. She lives near Princeton, New Jersey, loves to read and write, and is now cancer-free.

Amy Storms is a wife, mom, and freelance writer in Santa Clarita, California. An Oklahoma girl at heart, Amy lives with her pastor-husband Andy, their grade-school kids Nathan, Anne, and Molly, and a terribly unmotivated basset hound named Belle. Read more devotions from Amy at www.amystorms.com.

Ronica Stromberg has been a stay-at-home mom for fourteen years, raising two boys. Her humorous experiences with her sons inspired her to write many magazine articles and the bedtime book *The Time-for-Bed Angel*. She maintains a website at http://ronicastromberg.wordpress.com.

Letitia Suk loves to talk about personal renewal and family life. The author of *Rhythms of Renewal,* she is a life coach, a MOPS and retreat speaker, and a hospital chaplain (www.LetitiaSuk.com). She and her husband Tom live in Evanston, Illinois, and have four grown children and three perfect grandchildren.

Renee Swope is a national conference speaker, cohost of Proverbs 31 Ministries' international radio program, and author of *A Confident Heart: How to Stop Doubting Yourself and Live in the Security of God's Promises.* Her favorite titles are wife to JJ and mom to Joshua, seventeen, Andrew, fourteen, and Aster, three. Connect with Renee at www.ReneeSwope.com.

Leeana Tankersley is a writer and speaker. Her first book, *Found Art: Discovering Beauty in Foreign Places* (Zondervan, 2009), is a spiritual memoir of the year she lived in the middle east with her US Navy SEAL husband. Leeana and Steve have three-year-old twins, Luke and Lane, and are currently stationed in Bahrain. Follow Leeana at www.gypsyink.com.

Ann Voskamp is a wife of a full-time farmer, the mother of six, and the *New York Times* bestselling author of *One Thousand Gifts: A Dare to Live Fully Right Where You Are*. Ann's a columnist with DaySpring, with articles featured in *WORLD Magazine*, the *Huffington Post*, and *Christianity Today*, but what really matters? The words she simply lives. This convicts her. Every day, she writes of messy, amazing grace at www. aholyexperience.com.

Stephanie Walter lives in Columbia, Missouri, with husband Dusty and their three children, Kate, Claire, and Ben. After a refreshing period of being a stay-at-home mom, Stephanie embarked on a part-time career instructing online classes, and she is thankful for finding balance and joy in God's perfect plans.

Angie Weszely is president of Caris, a Christian pregnancy counseling agency in Chicago. With a teenage daughter and a preschool son, she knows firsthand the challenges of balancing family with career. This fuels her passion to support women facing unplanned pregnancies in ways that reflect God's heart.

Karen Wilber is a freelance writer and stay-at-home mom blessed with two active young boys. She juggles family life, Bible study, teaching, and writing by nurturing a sense of humor. She blogs insights from her family's frugal lifestyle at www.frugalfamilyfriend.com.

Lori Wurth and her husband were blessed with two more children, a biological son through IVF, and a daughter through adoption. Lori lives in Colorado where she stays at home with her children during the day, teaches college courses at night, and is actively involved in her church's MOPS group.

Acknowledgments

I was privileged to sit with the stories and struggles of mothers from across our nation and a few others. The devotions here represent hundreds of other women who took to keyboards to shine a light on God's abiding presence. Your journeys matter—to him and to me.

Thanks to Jean Blackmer and Carla Foote for their support and confidence. I am humbled by and grateful for the impact MOPS International has had on me as a person and a professional all these years.

All the words I write are inspired by the love of my life, Todd, and the miracles we chase around each day: Zach, Luke, and A.J. Thanks, guys, for encouraging me to exercise my writer's soul. And for giving me so much good material to do it with.

My God, against all odds, made me a mother. There aren't enough words to acknowledge what that means to me.

Susan Besze Wallace

Want to be the best mom possible?
You are not alone.

At MOPS you can enjoy real friendships,
personal growth, and spiritual hope
as part of a mothering community.

Get connected today!

Mothers of Preschoolers

2370 S. Trenton Way, Denver CO 80231
888.910.MOPS

For information on MOPS International, visit **MOPS.org**

Better Moms Make a Better World

Helping Moms Create Vibrant Relationships in the Midst of Motherhood

A mom's guide to creating vibrant friendships with other women that feed both their creativity and sense of purpose in the larger world.

Available Wherever Books Are Sold

 **Revell**
a division of Baker Publishing Group
www.RevellBooks.com

"Do yourself a favor and bathe in the wisdom of this book—you'll emerge with more confidence and strength in what every mom has inside: the power to be a great mother."

—Lisa T. Bergren, author, *Life on Planet Mom*

Helps a woman develop confidence in her parenting skills by equipping her with basic mothering strategies and teaching her to trust her intuition.

Available Wherever Books Are Sold

Revell
a division of Baker Publishing Group
www.RevellBooks.com

"I believe *Momology* is the most user-friendly, relevant, and complete resource for moms today."

—Carol Kuykendall, author of *Five-Star Families*

Mothering is part art, part science, and always a work in progress! Backed by more than thirty years of research-based ministry at MOPS International, *Momology* is designed to help you be the unique mother God created you to be—because better moms make a better world.

Available Wherever Books Are Sold

 Revell
a division of Baker Publis
www.RevellBooks.com